GEORGE HERBERT

100 POEMS

100
POEMS

George Herbert

SELECTED AND EDITED BY
Helen Wilcox

CAMBRIDGE
UNIVERSITY PRESS

CAMBRIDGE
UNIVERSITY PRESS

University Printing House, Cambridge CB2 8BS, United Kingdom

Cambridge University Press is part of the University of Cambridge.

It furthers the University's mission by disseminating knowledge in the pursuit of
education, learning and research at the highest international levels of excellence.

www.cambridge.org
Information on this title: www.cambridge.org/9781107151451

© Cambridge University Press 2016

First published 2016

Printed in the United States of America by Sheridan Books, Inc.

A catalogue record for this publication is available from the British Library

ISBN 978-1-107-15145-1 Hardback

Contents

Preface

HELEN WILCOX

Reading the poetry of George Herbert is like entering a room in which a conversation is going on, and finding oneself drawn unwittingly into the dialogue. The tenor of the conversation is very often loving, but it can also seem perplexed, disappointed or anxious, and sometimes angry. The main speaker frequently addresses God, though occasionally we hear the voice of the Lord in response, gently nudging the protesting human towards greater understanding. The speaker enters into debates with God, but also with parts of his own self – his wayward thoughts, his hard heart – and sometimes seems to recount stories for an audience. Above all, the voice of the speaker is so familiar in all its variety of moods and tones that we, as readers, can find our own experiences given expression in the poems, and we may in some sense become the speaker, too. Reading, and re-reading, Herbert's poems is a process of self-discovery.

How can this be said in the early twenty-first century about a devotional poet who was writing four centuries ago? The key to the immediacy and accessibility of Herbert's verse is its rare balance of rhetorical skill and complexity on the one hand, and a simplicity and directness of style on the other. The closing line of his last lyric is about as plain and monosyllabic a statement as one could utter: 'So I did sit and eat' ('Love (III)'). The power of the short line derives from its position, having been held back until the end of the poem after the sophisticated poetic dialogue and verbal dance that precede it; the impact of the line also stems from the layers of social and spiritual significance given during the poem to the act of eating. The lyric's remarkable clarity is thus an achieved simplicity, brought about by the writer's knowledge and craftsmanship. As Herbert writes in 'Praise (II)', the fresh spontaneity with which the feelings of the 'heart' are poured out is finely controlled by the poet's 'utmost art'.

Many modern readers come to Herbert's poetry through its association with another art form, music, whether the words are familiar as hymns or in musical settings for concert performance. This connection is most apt, for the poems themselves are profoundly musical: they frequently use the stanza forms of song lyrics, delight in rhyme and other forms of sonic 'chiming', identify their role as 'hymns' or 'window-songs' to God, widely employ musical metaphors and experience the process of praise as the heart's 'singing' ('Deniall', 'A true Hymne', 'Dulnesse', 'Easter'). This lyrical nature of Herbert's verse is a reminder of how greatly he was inspired by the Psalms, the biblical songs of David which similarly give voice to the whole spectrum of human emotions. Conscious of this intensely biblical quality of Herbert's poetry, one of his early readers referred to the poet as a new Psalmist, the 'incomparable sweet Singer of our Israel' (Oliver Heywood, *The Sure Mercies of David* (1672), p. 119).

By contrast, some of Herbert's poems are more notable for their visual impact than their lyrical sweetness. Again, the poet is using all his verbal art to give material expression to the spiritual life: words are to be seen as well as heard, and the shape of a poem on the page can contribute significantly to its meaning. Herbert's carefully constructed poems such as 'The Altar' or 'Easter wings' are the seventeenth-century equivalent of concrete poetry, showing how a 'broken' heart can still be moulded to form a place of offering ('The Altar'), or how necessary it is for the human spirit to become 'most thinne' before it can expand into flight with the risen Christ ('Easter wings'). Every dimension of language – what it looks like, how it sounds, what it recalls and what it means – is pressed into service by this most inventive of poets. He even discovers new meaning hidden within the constituent parts of words – expanding 'JESU' in the poem of the same name into the comforting phrase *'I ease you'*, for example – thus making the poet's task into a kind of re-spelling, re-interpreting the words and the world that we think we know so well.

Herbert is a poet of surprises: instead of resting our 'eye' on the surface of things, we are encouraged to look beyond and thus 'the heav'n espie' ('The Elixer'). A poem of deep spiritual frustration, such as 'Deniall', seems trapped in the misery of a disconsolate soul likened to an '[u]ntun'd, unstrung' musical instrument – yet even here there is an unexpected twist at the very end of the poem. The breakthrough comes when the speaker finally prays, in desperation, and immediately the last line restores both hope and a harmonious rhyme scheme. Verse structure and mood go hand in hand, and in a transformation that is a characteristic of Herbert's teasing titles, the denial which initially appeared to be God's refusal to hear the speaker turns out to have been the speaker's inability to admit God's love for him. The poems are fundamentally optimistic, yet never sentimental; they may be 'sweet', but their 'sweetness' derives from an exquisite rhetoric of spiritual honesty ('Jordan (II)'). Their hope is anchored in the resurrection, and their speakers take pleasure in the friendly companionship of the risen Christ, as a conversation partner or powerfully present in the bread and wine of the Eucharist. Typically, Herbert is repeatedly amazed by the generous humility of a God who offers himself as food to sustain his creation, not appearing with fanfare or grandeur but quietly 'creeping' into the human body 'by the way of nourishment and strength' ('The H. Communion').

An appreciation of Herbert's poetry is not at all dependent on knowledge of his life, but it is possible to see deep connections between the poet and his work. The finely poised skill of his verse should not be unexpected from the man who was public orator of Cambridge University in the early 1620s, and thus one of the most accomplished rhetoricians of his generation. The musical qualities of his poetry, too, may be linked to his reported love of hearing and playing music, both in church and at home. The elegant sociability of many of his poetic narrators is in keeping with the milieu of a man whose birth and achievements seemed to destine him for a career at court. Equally, the love of everyday images and plain phrases such as 'My God and King' ('Antiphon (I)') reveals the biblical grounding and pastoral sensitivity of the country parson he eventually became. Herbert's life and works are both full of paradoxes, each bringing together apparently opposing qualities in a way which makes his poetry fascinating and appealing, just as his lyrics manage to combine witty playfulness with deep seriousness and devotion. This is the poet who carefully devised subtle varieties of stanza and rhyme structure for each lyric that he wrote, in order to match most precisely the form to its meaning; yet at the same time this is a writer who was intensely aware of the temptation inherent in poetry's 'sweet phrases' and 'lovely metaphors' ('The Forerunners'). He was anxious to use beautiful language but always alert to the dangers of '[c]urling with metaphors a plain intention' ('Jordan (II)'), seeking instead to establish the 'beautie' intrinsic to 'truth' itself ('Jordan (I)').

Herbert died in 1633 at the age of forty, and his only volume of English verse, *The Temple*, was printed posthumously in the same year. With its engaging clarity and enticing skill, Herbert's poetry immediately became a best-seller. *The Temple* was published during a period of great religious tension in Britain, less than ten years before the outbreak of Civil War, yet the poems manage to wear their doctrinal loyalties so lightly that his work was popular among early readers as far apart politically as King Charles I and the chaplain to Oliver Cromwell. Like the Bible by which it is so profoundly influenced, Herbert's devotional verse became a kind of communal cultural property, and indeed continues to this day to inspire readers from a huge variety of backgrounds and affinities.

In its original form, Herbert's collection of poetry was in three parts: 'The Church-porch', 'The Church' (containing all his shorter English lyrics) and 'The Church Militant'. Unfortunately, there is insufficient room in this selection for the two longer poems which framed 'The Church' in its seventeenth-century social context. 'The Church-porch', a didactic poem concerned with how to live a worthy life, helped the reader over the threshold from the secular world into the sacred space of

'The Church', the appropriate location for the lyric poems focusing on spiritual and liturgical life. At the other end of the volume, 'The Church Militant' led the reader out of the church with a historic account of the struggle of the Christian faith around the world. Though this symbolic architectural vision of a church with its entrance and exit was obviously vital to the conception of Herbert's original volume, it is the shorter lyric poems which tend to speak most vividly to readers now and are therefore represented in this selection.

The task of choosing just 100 of Herbert's lyrics for this current volume, from over 160 poems in 'The Church', was unexpectedly challenging; the fact is that Herbert wrote many more than 100 excellent poems! Readers familiar with his work may regret, as I do, the exclusion of poems such as 'Time', 'Giddinesse', 'The Glimpse', 'The Rose' and 'The Banquet', and it was obviously a difficult decision to leave out one of his five 'Affliction' poems, or two of the three poems entitled 'Praise'. These sacrifices have been made, however, in order to present 100 poems which represent the range of forms, moods, subjects, tones and styles to be found among the lyrics of 'The Church'. The poems appear in the order in which they were printed in 1633, to highlight some of the deliberate thematic clusters featured in 'The Church' – the passion and Easter at the beginning of the sequence, for example; the church services, features and festivals towards the middle, and death and the afterlife at the end of the collection. The ups and downs of an individual's relationship with God are given vivid expression throughout 'The Church', and the aim of this selection is, as far as possible, to honour the immense richness of Herbert's poetic art and allow readers, as he phrases it in 'The Flower', to 'relish' his 'versing'. The work of the greatest devotional poet in the English language deserves no less.

THE DEDICATION

Lord, my first fruits present themselves to thee;
Yet not mine neither: for from thee they came,
And must return. Accept of them and me,
And make us strive, who shall sing best thy name.
5   Turn their eyes hither, who shall make a gain:
        Theirs, who shall hurt themselves or me, refrain.

THE ALTAR

A broken A L T A R, Lord, thy servant reares,
Made of a heart, and cemented with teares:
    Whose parts are as thy hand did frame;
    No workmans tool hath touch'd the same.
5   A H E A R T alone
          Is   such   a   stone,
          As   nothing   but
          Thy pow'r doth cut.
          Wherefore each part
10   Of my hard heart
          Meets in this frame,
          To praise thy name.
    That if I chance to hold my peace,
    These stones to praise thee may not cease.
15 O let thy blessed S A C R I F I C E be mine,
And sanctifie this A L T A R to be thine.

3

FROM THE SACRIFICE

Oh all ye, who passe by, whose eyes and minde
To worldly things are sharp, but to me blinde;
To me, who took eyes that I might you finde:
                    Was ever grief like mine?

...

Mine own Apostle, who the bag did beare,
Though he had all I had, did not forbeare
To sell me also, and to put me there:
                    Was ever grief like mine?

For thirtie pence he did my death devise,
Who at three hundred did the ointment prize,
Not half so sweet as my sweet sacrifice:
                    Was ever grief like mine?

Therefore my soul melts, and my hearts deare treasure
Drops bloud (the onely beads) my words to measure:
O let this cup passe, if it be thy pleasure:
                    Was ever grief like mine?

These drops being temper'd with a sinners tears,
A Balsome are for both the Hemispheres:
Curing all wounds, but mine; all, but my fears:
                    Was ever grief like mine?

Yet my Disciples sleep: I cannot gain
One houre of watching; but their drowsie brain
Comforts not me, and doth my doctrine stain:
                          Was ever grief like mine?

Arise, arise, they come. Look how they runne.
Alas! what haste they make to be undone!
How with their lanterns do they seek the sunne!
                          Was ever grief like mine?

With clubs and staves they seek me, as a thief,
Who am the way of truth, the true relief;
Most true to those, who are my greatest grief:
                          Was ever grief like mine?

Judas, dost thou betray me with a kisse?
Canst thou finde hell about my lips? and misse
Of life, just at the gates of life and blisse?
                          Was ever grief like mine?

                    . . .

O all ye who passe by, behold and see;
Man stole the fruit, but I must climbe the tree;
The tree of life to all, but onely me:
                          Was ever grief like mine?

Lo, here I hang, charg'd with a world of sinne,
The greater world o' th' two; for that came in
By words, but this by sorrow I must win:
                          Was ever grief like mine?

Such sorrow, as if sinfull man could feel,
210   Or feel his part, he would not cease to kneel,
Till all were melted, though he were all steel:
                         Was ever grief like mine?

But, *O my God, my God!* why leav'st thou me,
The sonne, in whom thou dost delight to be?
215   *My God, my God* ————
                         Never was grief like mine.

Shame tears my soul, my bodie many a wound;
Sharp nails pierce this, but sharper that confound;
Reproches, which are free, while I am bound.
220   Was ever grief like mine?

Now heal thy self, Physician; now come down.
Alas! I did so, when I left my crown
And fathers smile for you, to feel his frown:
                         Was ever grief like mine?

225   In healing not my self, there doth consist
All that salvation, which ye now resist;
Your safetie in my sicknesse doth subsist:
                         Was ever grief like mine?

Betwixt two theeves I spend my utmost breath,
230   As he that for some robberie suffereth.
Alas! what have I stollen from you? death:
                         Was ever grief like mine?

A king my title is, prefixt on high;
Yet by my subjects am condemn'd to die
A servile death in servile companie:
                              Was ever grief like mine?

They gave me vineger mingled with gall,
But more with malice: yet, when they did call,
With Manna, Angels food, I fed them all:
                              Was ever grief like mine?

They part my garments, and by lot dispose
My coat, the type of love, which once cur'd those
Who sought for help, never malicious foes:
                              Was ever grief like mine?

Nay, after death their spite shall further go;
For they will pierce my side, I full well know;
That as sinne came, so Sacraments might flow:
                              Was ever grief like mine?

But now I die; now all is finished.
My wo, mans weal: and now I bow my head.
Onely let others say, when I am dead,
                              Never was grief like mine.

Lines quoted are 1–4, 13–44, 201–52

6

4

THE THANKSGIVING

Oh King of grief! (a title strange, yet true,
  To thee of all kings onely due)
Oh King of wounds! how shall I grieve for thee,
  Who in all grief preventest me?
5 Shall I weep bloud? why thou hast wept such store
  That all thy body was one doore.
Shall I be scourged, flouted, boxed, sold?
  'Tis but to tell the tale is told.
My God, my God, why dost thou part from me?
10 Was such a grief as cannot be.
Shall I then sing, skipping, thy dolefull storie,
  And side with thy triumphant glorie?
Shall thy strokes be my stroking? thorns, my flower?
  Thy rod, my posie? crosse, my bower?
15 But how then shall I imitate thee, and
  Copie thy fair, though bloudie hand?
Surely I will reuenge me on thy love,
  And trie who shall victorious prove.
If thou dost give me wealth; I will restore
20 All back unto thee by the poore.
If thou dost give me honour; men shall see,
  The honour doth belong to thee.
I will not marry; or, if she be mine,
  She and her children shall be thine.
25 My bosome friend, if he blaspheme thy name,
  I will tear thence his love and fame.
One half of me being gone, the rest I give
  Unto some Chappell, die or live.

As for thy passion — But of that anon,
30   When with the other I have done.
For thy predestination I'le contrive,
    That three yeares hence, if I survive,
I'le build a spittle, or mend common wayes,
    But mend mine own without delayes.
35 Then I will use the works of thy creation,
    As if I us'd them but for fashion.
The world and I will quarrell; and the yeare
    Shall not perceive, that I am here.
My musick shall finde thee, and ev'ry string
40   Shall have his attribute to sing;
That all together may accord in thee,
    And prove one God, one harmonie.
If thou shalt give me wit, it shall appeare,
    If thou hast giv'n it me, 'tis here.
45 Nay, I will reade thy book, and never move
    Till I have found therein thy love;
Thy art of love, which I'le turn back on thee,
    O my deare Saviour, Victorie!
Then for thy passion – I will do for that –
50   Alas, my God, I know not what.

5

THE AGONIE

Philosophers have measur'd mountains,
Fathom'd the depths of seas, of states, and kings,
Walk'd with a staffe to heav'n, and traced fountains:
      But there are two vast, spacious things,
5   The which to measure it doth more behove:
Yet few there are that sound them; Sinne and Love.

      Who would know Sinne, let him repair
Unto mount Olivet; there shall he see
A man so wrung with pains, that all his hair,
10   His skinne, his garments bloudie be.
Sinne is that presse and vice, which forceth pain
To hunt his cruell food through ev'ry vein.

      Who knows not Love, let him assay
And taste that juice, which on the crosse a pike
15   Did set again abroach; then let him say
      If ever he did taste the like.
Love is that liquour sweet and most divine,
Which my God feels as bloud; but I, as wine.

6

GOOD FRIDAY

※

O my chief good,
How shall I measure out thy bloud?
How shall I count what thee befell,
      And each grief tell?

5   Shall I thy woes
Number according to thy foes?
Or, since one starre show'd thy first breath,
      Shall all thy death?

          Or shall each leaf,
10   Which falls in Autumne, score a grief?
Or cannot leaves, but fruit, be signe
      Of the true vine?

          Then let each houre
Of my whole life one grief devoure;
15   That thy distresse through all may runne,
      And be my sunne.

          Or rather let
My severall sinnes their sorrows get;
That as each beast his cure doth know,
20   Each sinne may so.

Since bloud is fittest, Lord, to write
Thy sorrows in, and bloudie fight;
My heart hath store, write there, where in
One box doth lie both ink and sinne:

25   That when sinne spies so many foes,
Thy whips, thy nails, thy wounds, thy woes,
All come to lodge there, sinne may say,
No room for me, and flie away.

Sinne being gone, oh fill the place,
30   And keep possession with thy grace;
Lest sinne take courage and return,
And all the writings blot or burn.

7

REDEMPTION

Having been tenant long to a rich Lord,
      Not thriving, I resolved to be bold,
      And make a suit unto him, to afford
A new small-rented lease, and cancell th' old.

5   In heaven at his manour I him sought:
      They told me there, that he was lately gone
      About some land, which he had dearly bought
Long since on earth, to take possession.

I straight return'd, and knowing his great birth,
10   Sought him accordingly in great resorts;
      In cities, theatres, gardens, parks, and courts:
At length I heard a ragged noise and mirth

      Of theeves and murderers: there I him espied,
      Who straight, *Your suit is granted,* said, & died.

8

SEPULCHRE

O blessed bodie! Whither art thou thrown?
No lodging for thee, but a cold hard stone?
So many hearts on earth, and yet not one
                Receive thee?

5   Sure there is room within our hearts good store;
For they can lodge transgressions by the score:
Thousands of toyes dwell there, yet out of doore
                They leave thee.

But that which shews them large, shews them unfit.
10   What ever sinne did this pure rock commit,
Which holds thee now? Who hath indited it
                Of murder?

Where our hard hearts have took up stones to brain thee,
And missing this, most falsly did arraigne thee;
15   Onely these stones in quiet entertain thee,
                And order.

And as of old, the law by heav'nly art
Was writ in stone; so thou, which also art
The letter of the word, find'st no fit heart
20   To hold thee.

Yet do we still persist as we began,
And so should perish, but that nothing can,
Though it be cold, hard, foul, from loving man
                Withhold thee.

9

EASTER

Rise heart; thy Lord is risen. Sing his praise
                         Without delayes,
Who takes thee by the hand, that thou likewise
                         With him mayst rise:
5   That, as his death calcined thee to dust,
His life may make thee gold, and much more just.

Awake, my lute, and struggle for thy part
                         With all thy art.
The crosse taught all wood to resound his name,
10   Who bore the same.
His streched sinews taught all strings, what key
Is best to celebrate this most high day.

Consort both heart and lute, and twist a song
                         Pleasant and long:
15   Or since all musick is but three parts vied
                         And multiplied;
O let thy blessed Spirit bear a part,
And make up our defects with his sweet art.

I got me flowers to straw thy way;
20   I got me boughs off many a tree:
But thou wast up by break of day,
And brought'st thy sweets along with thee.

The Sunne arising in the East,
Though he give light, & th' East perfume;
25   If they should offer to contest
With thy arising, they presume.

Can there be any day but this,
Though many sunnes to shine endeavour?
We count three hundred, but we misse:
30   There is but one, and that one ever.

EASTER WINGS

My tender age in sorrow did beginne:
And still with sicknesses and shame
Thou didst so punish sinne,
That I became
Most thinne.
With
thee
Let me combine,
And feel this day thy victorie:
For, if I imp my wing on thine,
Affliction shall advance the flight in me.

Lord, who createdst man in wealth and store,
Though foolishly he lost the same,
Decaying more and more,
Till he became
Most poore:
With
thee
O let me rise
As larks, harmoniously,
And sing this day thy victories:
Then shall the fall further the flight in me.

5

10

15

20

H. BAPTISME (11)

Since, Lord, to thee
A narrow way and little gate
Is all the passage, on my infancie
Thou didst lay hold, and antedate
5   My faith in me.

O let me still
Write thee great God, and me a childe:
Let me be soft and supple to thy will,
Small to my self, to others milde,
10   Behither ill.

Although by stealth
My flesh get on, yet let her sister
My soul bid nothing, but preserve her wealth:
The growth of flesh is but a blister;
15   Childhood is health.

SINNE (I)

Lord, with what care hast thou begirt us round!
    Parents first season us: then schoolmasters
    Deliver us to laws; they send us bound
To rules of reason, holy messengers,

5 Pulpits and sundayes, sorrow dogging sinne,
    Afflictions sorted, anguish of all sizes,
    Fine nets and stratagems to catch us in,
Bibles laid open, millions of surprises,

Blessings beforehand, tyes of gratefulnesse,
10   The sound of glorie ringing in our eares:
        Without, our shame; within, our consciences;
Angels and grace, eternall hopes and fears.

        Yet all these fences and their whole aray
        One cunning bosome-sinne blows quite away.

13

AFFLICTION (1)

When first thou didst entice to thee my heart,
     I thought the service brave:
So many joyes I writ down for my part,
     Besides what I might have
5 Out of my stock of naturall delights,
Augmented with thy gracious benefits.

I looked on thy furniture so fine,
     And made it fine to me:
Thy glorious houshold-stuffe did me entwine,
10   And 'tice me unto thee.
Such starres I counted mine: both heav'n and earth
Payd me my wages in a world of mirth.

What pleasures could I want, whose King I served?
     Where joyes my fellows were.
15 Thus argu'd into hopes, my thoughts reserved
     No place for grief or fear.
Therefore my sudden soul caught at the place,
And made her youth and fiercenesse seek thy face.

At first thou gav'st me milk and sweetnesses;
20   I had my wish and way:
My dayes were straw'd with flow'rs and happinesse;
     There was no moneth but May.
But with my yeares sorrow did twist and grow,
And made a partie unawares for wo.

25   My flesh began unto my soul in pain,
                        Sicknesses cleave my bones;
    Consuming agues dwell in ev'ry vein,
                        And tune my breath to grones.
    Sorrow was all my soul; I scarce beleeved,
30   Till grief did tell me roundly, that I lived.

    When I got health, thou took'st away my life,
                        And more; for my friends die:
    My mirth and edge was lost; a blunted knife
                        Was of more use then I.
35   Thus thinne and lean without a fence or friend,
    I was blown through with ev'ry storm and winde.

    Whereas my birth and spirit rather took
                        The way that takes the town;
    Thou didst betray me to a lingring book,
40   And wrap me in a gown.
    I was entangled in the world of strife,
    Before I had the power to change my life.

    Yet, for I threatned oft the siege to raise,
                       Not simpring all mine age,
45   Thou often didst with Academick praise
                       Melt and dissolve my rage.
    I took thy sweetned pill, till I came neare;
    I could not go away, nor persevere.

Yet lest perchance I should too happie be
In my unhappinesse,

Turning my purge to food, thou throwest me
Into more sicknesses.

Thus doth thy power crosse-bias me, not making
Thine own gift good, yet me from my wayes taking.

Now I am here, what thou wilt do with me
None of my books will show.

I reade, and sigh, and wish I were a tree;
For sure then I should grow

To fruit or shade: at least some bird would trust
Her houshold to me, and I should be just.

Yet, though thou troublest me, I must be meek;
In weaknesse must be stout.

Well, I will change the service, and go seek
Some other master out.

Ah my deare God! though I am clean forgot,
Let me not love thee, if I love thee not.

14

REPENTANCE

Lord, I confesse my sinne is great;
Great is my sinne: Oh! gently treat
With thy quick flow'r, thy momentanie bloom;
   Whose life still pressing
5   Is one undressing,
A steadie aiming at a tombe.

Mans age is two houres work, or three:
Each day doth round about us see.
Thus are we to delights: but we are all
10   To sorrows old,
    If life be told
From what life feeleth, Adams fall.

O let thy height of mercie then
Compassionate short-breathed men.
15 Cut me not off for my most foul transgression:
    I do confesse
    My foolishnesse;
My God, accept of my confession.

Sweeten at length this bitter bowl,
20 Which thou hast pour'd into my soul;
Thy wormwood turn to health, windes to fair weather:
    For if thou stay,
    I and this day,
As we did rise, we die together.

25   When thou for sinne rebukest man,
            Forthwith he waxeth wo and wan:
       Bitternesse fills our bowels; all our hearts
                 Pine, and decay,
                 And drop away,
30   And carrie with them th' other parts.

          But thou wilt sinne and grief destroy;
           That so the broken bones may joy,
      And tune together in a well-set song,
                Full of his praises,
35   Who dead men raises.
       Fractures well cur'd make us more strong.

15

PRAYER (I)

Prayer the Churches banquet, Angels age,
      Gods breath in man returning to his birth,
      The soul in paraphrase, heart in pilgrimage,
The Christian plummet sounding heav'n and earth;

5 Engine against th' Almightie, sinners towre,
      Reversed thunder, Christ-side-piercing spear,
      The six-daies world transposing in an houre,
A kinde of tune, which all things heare and fear;

Softnesse, and peace, and joy, and love, and blisse,
10   Exalted Manna, gladnesse of the best,
      Heaven in ordinarie, man well drest,
The milkie way, the bird of Paradise,

      Church-bels beyond the starres heard, the souls bloud,
      The land of spices; something understood.

THE H. COMMUNION

Not in rich furniture, or fine aray,
            Nor in a wedge of gold,
            Thou, who from me wast sold,
    To me dost now thy self convey;
5   For so thou should'st without me still have been,
            Leaving within me sinne:

But by the way of nourishment and strength
            Thou creep'st into my breast;
            Making thy way my rest,
10   And thy small quantities my length;
    Which spread their forces into every part,
            Meeting sinnes force and art.

Yet can these not get over to my soul,
            Leaping the wall that parts
15   Our souls and fleshly hearts;
        But as th' outworks, they may controll
    My rebel-flesh, and carrying thy name,
            Affright both sinne and shame.

Onely thy grace, which with these elements comes,
20   Knoweth the ready way,
            And hath the privie key,
        Op'ning the souls most subtile rooms;
    While those to spirits refin'd, at doore attend
            Dispatches from their friend.

25   Give me my captive soul, or take
             My bodie also thither.
      Another lift like this will make
             Them both to be together.

      Before that sinne turn'd flesh to stone,
30   And all our lump to leaven;
      A fervent sigh might well have blown
             Our innocent earth to heaven.

      For sure when Adam did not know
             To sinne; or sinne to smother;
35   He might to heav'n from Paradise go,
             As from one room t'another.

      Thou hast restor'd us to this ease
             By this thy heav'nly bloud;
      Which I can go to, when I please,
40   And leave th' earth to their food.

ANTIPHON (I)

Cho. Let all the world in ev'ry corner sing,
My God and King.

Vers. The heav'ns are not too high,
His praise may thither flie:
5   The earth is not too low,
His praises there may grow.

Cho. Let all the world in ev'ry corner sing,
My God and King.

Vers. The church with psalms must shout,
10   No doore can keep them out:
But above all, the heart
Must bear the longest part.

Cho. Let all the world in ev'ry corner sing,
My God and King.

18

LOVE I AND II

I

Immortall Love, authour of this great frame,
    Sprung from that beautie which can never fade;
    How hath man parcel'd out thy glorious name,
And thrown it on that dust which thou hast made,

5   While mortall love doth all the title gain!
    Which siding with invention, they together
    Bear all the sway, possessing heart and brain,
(Thy workmanship) and give thee share in neither.

Wit fancies beautie, beautie raiseth wit:
10   The world is theirs; they two play out the game,
    Thou standing by: and though thy glorious name
Wrought our deliverance from th' infernall pit,

    Who sings thy praise? onely a skarf or glove
    Doth warm our hands, and make them write of love.

II

Immortall Heat, O let thy greater flame
    Attract the lesser to it: let those fires,
    Which shall consume the world, first make it tame;
And kindle in our hearts such true desires,

5   As may consume our lusts, and make thee way.
    Then shall our hearts pant thee; then shall our brain
    All her invention on thine Altar lay,
And there in hymnes send back thy fire again.

Our eies shall see thee, which before saw dust;
10   Dust blown by wit, till that they both were blinde:
    Thou shalt recover all thy goods in kinde,
Who wert disseized by usurping lust:

    All knees shall bow to thee; all wits shall rise,
    And praise him who did make and mend our eies.

THE TEMPER (1)

How should I praise thee, Lord! how should my rymes
    Gladly engrave thy love in steel,
    If what my soul doth feel sometimes,
        My soul might ever feel!

5   Although there were some fourtie heav'ns, or more,
    Sometimes I peere above them all;
    Sometimes I hardly reach a score,
        Sometimes to hell I fall.

O rack me not to such a vast extent;
10   Those distances belong to thee:
    The world's too little for thy tent,
        A grave too big for me.

Wilt thou meet arms with man, that thou dost stretch
    A crumme of dust from heav'n to hell?
15   Will great God measure with a wretch?
        Shall he thy stature spell?

O let me, when thy roof my soul hath hid,
    O let me roost and nestle there:
    Then of a sinner thou art rid,
20   And I of hope and fear.

Yet take thy way; for sure thy way is best:
    Stretch or contract me thy poore debter:
  This is but tuning of my breast,
      To make the musick better.

25   Whether I flie with angels, fall with dust,
    Thy hands made both, and I am there:
    Thy power and love, my love and trust
      Make one place ev'ry where.

JORDAN (1)

Who sayes that fictions onely and false hair
Become a verse? Is there in truth no beautie?
Is all good structure in a winding stair?
May no lines passe, except they do their dutie
5   Not to a true, but painted chair?

Is it no verse, except enchanted groves
And sudden arbours shadow course-spunne lines?
Must purling streams refresh a lovers loves?
Must all be vail'd, while he that reades, divines,
10   Catching the sense at two removes?

Shepherds are honest people; let them sing:
Riddle who list, for me, and pull for Prime:
I envie no mans nightingale or spring;
Nor let them punish me with losse of ryme,
15   Who plainly say, *My God, My King.*

EMPLOYMENT (1)

If as a flowre doth spread and die,
　　Thou wouldst extend me to some good,
Before I were by frosts extremitie
　　　　　　Nipt in the bud;

5　　　The sweetnesse and the praise were thine;
　　But the extension and the room,
Which in thy garland I should fill, were mine
　　　　　　At thy great doom.

For as thou dost impart thy grace,
10　　The greater shall our glorie be.
The measure of our joyes is in this place,
　　　　　　The stuffe with thee.

Let me not languish then, and spend
　　A life as barren to thy praise,
15　As is the dust, to which that life doth tend,
　　　　　　But with delaies.

All things are busie; onely I
　　Neither bring hony with the bees,
Nor flowres to make that, nor the husbandrie
20　　　　　　To water these.

I am no link of thy great chain,
　　But all my companie is a weed.
Lord place me in thy consort; give one strain
　　　　　　To my poore reed.

THE H. SCRIPTURES I AND II

I

Oh Book! infinite sweetnesse! let my heart
    Suck ev'ry letter, and a hony gain,
    Precious for any grief in any part;
To cleare the breast, to mollifie all pain.

5   Thou art all health, health thriving, till it make
        A full eternitie: thou art a masse
        Of strange delights, where we may wish & take.
Ladies, look here; this is the thankfull glasse,

That mends the lookers eyes: this is the well
10   That washes what it shows. Who can indeare
        Thy praise too much? thou art heav'ns Lidger here,
Working against the states of death and hell.

        Thou art joyes handsell: heav'n lies flat in thee,
        Subject to ev'ry mounters bended knee.

II

Oh that I knew how all thy lights combine,
      And the configurations of their glorie!
      Seeing not onely how each verse doth shine,
But all the constellations of the storie.

5   This verse marks that, and both do make a motion
      Unto a third, that ten leaves off doth lie:
      Then as dispersed herbs do watch a potion,
These three make up some Christians destinie:

Such are thy secrets, which my life makes good,
10   And comments on thee: for in ev'ry thing
      Thy words do finde me out, & parallels bring,
And in another make me understood.

      Starres are poore books, & oftentimes do misse:
      This book of starres lights to eternall blisse.

WHITSUNDAY

※

Listen sweet Dove unto my song,
And spread thy golden wings in me;
Hatching my tender heart so long,
Till it get wing, and flie away with thee.

5   Where is that fire which once descended
On thy Apostles? thou didst then
Keep open house, richly attended,
Feasting all comers by twelve chosen men.

   Such glorious gifts thou didst bestow,
10 That th' earth did like a heav'n appeare;
The starres were coming down to know
If they might mend their wages, and serve here.

   The sunne, which once did shine alone,
Hung down his head, and wisht for night,
15 When he beheld twelve sunnes for one
Going about the world, and giving light.

   But since those pipes of gold, which brought
That cordiall water to our ground,
Were cut and martyr'd by the fault
20 Of those, who did themselves through their side wound,

Thou shutt'st the doore, and keep'st within;
Scarce a good joy creeps through the chink:
And if the braves of conqu'ring sinne
Did not excite thee, we should wholly sink.

25   Lord, though we change, thou art the same;
The same sweet God of love and light:
Restore this day, for thy great name,
Unto his ancient and miraculous right.

24

GRACE

❦

My stock lies dead, and no increase
Doth my dull husbandrie improve:
O let thy graces without cease
                Drop from above!

5   If still the sunne should hide his face,
Thy house would but a dungeon prove,
Thy works nights captives: O let grace
                Drop from above!

The dew doth ev'ry morning fall;
10   And shall the dew out-strip thy dove?
The dew, for which grasse cannot call,
                Drop from above.

Death is still working like a mole,
And digs my grave at each remove:
15   Let grace work too, and on my soul
                Drop from above.

Sinne is still hammering my heart
Unto a hardnesse, void of love:
Let suppling grace, to crosse his art,
20   Drop from above.

O come! for thou dost know the way.
Or if to me thou wilt not move,
Remove me, where I need not say,
                Drop from above.

25

MATTENS

I cannot ope mine eyes,
But thou art ready there to catch
My morning-soul and sacrifice:
Then we must needs for that day make a match.

5   My God, what is a heart?
Silver, or gold, or precious stone,
Or starre, or rainbow, or a part
Of all these things, or all of them in one?

My God, what is a heart,
10   That thou shouldst it so eye, and wooe,
Powring upon it all thy art,
As if that thou hadst nothing els to do?

Indeed mans whole estate
Amounts (and richly) to serve thee:
15   He did not heav'n and earth create,
Yet studies them, not him by whom they be.

Teach me thy love to know;
That this new light, which now I see,
May both the work and workman show:
20   Then by a sunne-beam I will climbe to thee.

EVEN-SONG

Blest be the God of love,
Who gave me eyes, and light, and power this day,
Both to be busie, and to play.
But much more blest be God above,

5   Who gave me sight alone,
Which to himself he did denie:
For when he sees my waies, I dy:
But I have got his sonne, and he hath none.

What have I brought thee home
10   For this thy love? have I discharg'd the debt,
Which this dayes favour did beget?
I ranne; but all I brought, was fome.

Thy diet, care, and cost
Do end in bubbles, balls of winde;
15   Of winde to thee whom I have crost,
But balls of wilde-fire to my troubled minde.

Yet still thou goest on,
And now with darknesse closest wearie eyes,
Saying to man, *It doth suffice :*
20   *Henceforth repose; your work is done.*

Thus in thy Ebony box
Thou dost inclose us, till the day
Put our amendment in our way,
And give new wheels to our disorder'd clocks.

<pre>
25   I muse, which shows more love,
        The day or night: that is the gale, this th'harbour;
                        That is the walk, and this the arbour;
                        Or that the garden, this the grove.

                        My God, thou art all love.
30   Not one poore minute scapes thy breast,
                        But brings a favour from above;
        And in this love, more then in bed, I rest.
</pre>

CHURCH-MONUMENTS

While that my soul repairs to her devotion,
Here I intombe my flesh, that it betimes
May take acquaintance of this heap of dust;
To which the blast of deaths incessant motion,
Fed with the exhalation of our crimes,
Drives all at last. Therefore I gladly trust

My bodie to this school, that it may learn
To spell his elements, and finde his birth
Written in dustie heraldrie and lines;
Which dissolution sure doth best discern,
Comparing dust with dust, and earth with earth.
These laugh at Ieat, and Marble put for signes,

To sever the good fellowship of dust,
And spoil the meeting. What shall point out them,
When they shall bow, and kneel, and fall down flat
To kisse those heaps, which now they have in trust?
Deare flesh, while I do pray, learn here thy stemme
And true descent; that when thou shalt grow fat,

And wanton in thy cravings, thou mayst know,
That flesh is but the glasse, which holds the dust
That measures all our time; which also shall
Be crumbled into dust. Mark here below
How tame these ashes are, how free from lust,
That thou mayst fit thy self against thy fall.

28

CHURCH-MUSICK

Sweetest of sweets, I thank you: when displeasure
    Did through my bodie wound my minde,
You took me thence, and in your house of pleasure
    A daintie lodging me assign'd.

5   Now I in you without a bodie move,
    Rising and falling with your wings:
We both together sweetly live and love,
    Yet say sometimes, *God help poore Kings.*

Comfort, I'le die; for if you poste from me,
10   Sure I shall do so, and much more:
But if I travell in your companie,
    You know the way to heavens doore.

THE CHURCH-FLOORE

꜒꜒

Mark you the floore? that square & speckled stone,
   Which looks so firm and strong,
     Is *Patience:*

And th' other black and grave, wherewith each one
5   Is checker'd all along,
      Humilitie:

The gentle rising, which on either hand
    Leads to the Quire above,
      Is *Confidence:*

10 But the sweet cement, which in one sure band
    Ties the whole frame, is *Love*
      And *Charitie.*

   Hither sometimes Sinne steals, and stains
   The marbles neat and curious veins:
15 But all is cleansed when the marble weeps.
   Sometimes Death, puffing at the doore,
   Blows all the dust about the floore:
But while he thinks to spoil the room, he sweeps.
   Blest be the *Architect*, whose art
20   Could build so strong in a weak heart.

THE WINDOWS

Lord, how can man preach thy eternall word?
        He is a brittle crazie glasse:
Yet in thy temple thou dost him afford
        This glorious and transcendent place,
5   To be a window, through thy grace.

But when thou dost anneal in glasse thy storie,
        Making thy life to shine within
The holy Preachers; then the light and glorie
        More rev'rend grows, & more doth win:
10   Which else shows watrish, bleak, & thin.

Doctrine and life, colours and light, in one
        When they combine and mingle, bring
A strong regard and aw: but speech alone
        Doth vanish like a flaring thing,
15   And in the eare, not conscience ring.

TRINITIE SUNDAY

Lord, who hast form'd me out of mud,
    And hast redeem'd me through thy bloud,
    And sanctifi'd me to do good;

Purge all my sinnes done heretofore:
    For I confesse my heavie score,
    And I will strive to sinne no more.

Enrich my heart, mouth, hands in me,
    With faith, with hope, with charitie;
    That I may runne, rise, rest with thee.

32

CONTENT

Peace mutt'ring thoughts, and do not grudge to keep
      Within the walls of your own breast:
Who cannot on his own bed sweetly sleep,
      Can on anothers hardly rest.

5   Gad not abroad at ev'ry quest and call
      Of an untrained hope or passion.
To court each place or fortune that doth fall,
      Is wantonnesse in contemplation.

Mark how the fire in flints doth quiet lie,
10   Content and warm t' it self alone:
But when it would appeare to others eye,
      Without a knock it never shone.

Give me the pliant minde, whose gentle measure
      Complies and suits with all estates;
15 Which can let loose to a crown, and yet with pleasure
      Take up within a cloisters gates.

This soul doth span the world, and hang content
      From either pole unto the centre:
Where in each room of the well-furnisht tent
20   He lies warm, and without adventure.

The brags of life are but a nine dayes wonder;
      And after death the fumes that spring
From private bodies, make as big a thunder,
      As those which rise from a huge King.

25 Onely thy Chronicle is lost; and yet
            Better by worms be all once spent,
Then to have hellish moths still gnaw and fret
            Thy name in books, which may not rent:

When all thy deeds, whose brunt thou feel'st alone,
30   Are chaw'd by others pens and tongue;
And as their wit is, their digestion,
            Thy nourisht fame is weak or strong.

Then cease discoursing soul, till thine own ground,
            Do not thy self or friends importune.
35 He that by seeking hath himself once found,
            Hath euer found a happie fortune.

33

THE QUIDDITIE

My God, a verse is not a crown,
No point of honour, or gay suit,
No hawk, or banquet, or renown,
Nor a good sword, nor yet a lute:

5 It cannot vault, or dance, or play;
It never was in *France* or *Spain*;
Nor can it entertain the day
With a great stable or demain:

It is no office, art, or news,
10 Nor the Exchange, or busie Hall;
But it is that which while I use
I am with thee, and *Most take all.*

34

AFFLICTION (III)

My heart did heave, and there came forth, *O God!*
By that I knew that thou wast in the grief,
To guide and govern it to my relief,
      Making a scepter of the rod:
5   Hadst thou not had thy part,
Sure the unruly sigh had broke my heart.

But since thy breath gave me both life and shape,
Thou knowst my tallies; and when there's assign'd
So much breath to a sigh, what's then behinde?
10   Or if some yeares with it escape,
          The sigh then onely is
A gale to bring me sooner to my blisse.

Thy life on earth was grief, and thou art still
Constant unto it, making it to be
15 A point of honour, now to grieve in me,
      And in thy members suffer ill.
          They who lament one crosse,
Thou dying dayly, praise thee to thy losse.

35

THE STARRE

Bright spark, shot from a brighter place,
  Where beams surround my Saviours face,
   Canst thou be any where
    So well as there?

5 Yet, if thou wilt from thence depart,
  Take a bad lodging in my heart;
   For thou canst make a debter,
    And make it better.

First with thy fire-work burn to dust
10 Folly, and worse then folly, lust:
   Then with thy light refine,
    And make it shine:

So disengag'd from sinne and sicknesse,
  Touch it with thy celestiall quicknesse,
15 That it may hang and move
    After thy love.

Then with our trinitie of light,
  Motion, and heat, let's take our flight
   Unto the place where thou
20 Before didst bow.

Get me a standing there, and place
  Among the beams, which crown the face
   Of him, who dy'd to part
    Sinne and my heart:

That so among the rest I may
   Glitter, and curle, and winde as they:
    That winding is their fashion
     Of adoration.

Sure thou wilt joy, by gaining me
   To flie home like a laden bee
    Unto that hive of beams
     And garland-streams.

36

TO ALL ANGELS AND SAINTS

Oh glorious spirits, who after all your bands
See the smooth face of God, without a frown
            Or strict commands;
Where ev'ry one is king, and hath his crown,
5   If not upon his head, yet in his hands:

Not out of envie or maliciousnesse
Do I forbear to crave your speciall aid:
            I would addresse
My vows to thee most gladly, blessed Maid,
10   And Mother of my God, in my distresse.

Thou art the holy mine, whence came the gold,
The great restorative for all decay
            In young and old;
Thou art the cabinet where the jewell lay:
15   Chiefly to thee would I my soul unfold:

But now (alas!) I dare not; for our King,
Whom we do all joyntly adore and praise,
            Bids no such thing:
And where his pleasure no injunction layes,
20   ('Tis your own case) ye never move a wing.

All worship is prerogative, and a flower
Of his rich crown, from whom lyes no appeal
            At the last houre:
Therefore we dare not from his garland steal,
25   To make a posie for inferiour power.

Although then others court you, if ye know
What's done on earth, we shall not fare the worse,
            Who do not so;
Since we are ever ready to disburse,
If any one our Masters hand can show.

30

37

DENIALL

When my devotions could not pierce
                    Thy silent eares;
Then was my heart broken, as was my verse:
                    My breast was full of fears
5   And disorder:

My bent thoughts, like a brittle bow,
                    Did flie asunder:
Each took his way; some would to pleasures go,
                    Some to the warres and thunder
10   Of alarms.

As good go any where, they say,
                    As to benumme
Both knees and heart, in crying night and day,
                    Come, come, my God, O come,
15   But no hearing.

O that thou shouldst give dust a tongue
                    To crie to thee,
And then not heare it crying! all day long
                    My heart was in my knee,
20   But no hearing.

Therefore my soul lay out of sight,
                    Untun'd, unstrung:
My feeble spirit, unable to look right,
                    Like a nipt blossome, hung
25   Discontented.

O cheer and tune my heartlesse breast,
                    Deferre no time;
That so thy favours granting my request,
                    They and my minde may chime,
                              And mend my ryme.

38

CHRISTMAS

All after pleasures as I rid one day,
  My horse and I, both tir'd, bodie and minde,
  With full crie of affections, quite astray;
I took up in the next inne I could finde.

5 There when I came, whom found I but my deare,
  My dearest Lord, expecting till the grief
  Of pleasures brought me to him, readie there
To be all passengers most sweet relief?

O thou, whose glorious, yet contracted light,
10 Wrapt in nights mantle, stole into a manger;
  Since my dark soul and brutish is thy right,
To Man of all beasts be not thou a stranger:

  Furnish & deck my soul, that thou mayst have
  A better lodging, then a rack, or grave.

15 The shepherds sing; and shall I silent be?
   My God, no hymne for thee?
My soul's a shepherd too; a flock it feeds
   Of thoughts, and words, and deeds.
The pasture is thy word: the streams, thy grace
20   Enriching all the place.
Shepherd and flock shall sing, and all my powers
   Out-sing the day-light houres.
Then we will chide the sunne for letting night
   Take up his place and right:

25 We sing one common Lord; wherefore he should
                    Himself the candle hold.
    I will go searching, till I find a sunne
                    Shall stay, till we have done;
    A willing shiner, that shall shine as gladly,
30   As frost-nipt sunnes look sadly.
    Then we will sing, and shine all our own day,
                    And one another pay:
    His beams shall cheer my breast, and both so twine,
    Till ev'n his beams sing, and my musick shine.

39

UNGRATEFULNESSE

Lord, with what bountie and rare clemencie
      Hast thou redeem'd us from the grave!
          If thou hadst let us runne,
        Gladly had man ador'd the sunne,
5   And thought his god most brave;
Where now we shall be better gods then he.

Thou hast but two rare cabinets full of treasure,
      The *Trinitie*, and *Incarnation*:
          Thou hast unlockt them both,
10   And made them jewels to betroth
          The work of thy creation
Unto thy self in everlasting pleasure.

The statelier cabinet is the *Trinitie*,
      Whose sparkling light accesse denies:
15   Therefore thou dost not show
        This fully to us, till death blow
          The dust into our eyes:
For by that powder thou wilt make us see.

But all thy sweets are packt up in the other;
20   Thy mercies thither flock and flow:
          That as the first affrights,
        This may allure us with delights;
          Because this box we know;
For we have all of us just such another.

25 But man is close, reserv'd, and dark to thee:
When thou demandest but a heart,
He cavils instantly.
In his poore cabinet of bone
Sinnes have their box apart,
30 Defrauding thee, who gavest two for one.

40

SIGHS AND GRONES

O do not use me
After my sinnes! look not on my desert,
But on thy glorie! then thou wilt reform
And not refuse me: for thou onely art
5   The mightie God, but I a sillie worm;
            O do not bruise me!

O do not urge me!
For what account can thy ill steward make?
I have abus'd thy stock, destroy'd thy woods,
10   Suckt all thy magazens: my head did ake,
Till it found out how to consume thy goods:
            O do not scourge me!

O do not blinde me!
I have deserv'd that an Egyptian night
15   Should thicken all my powers; because my lust
Hath still sow'd fig-leaves to exclude thy light:
But I am frailtie, and already dust;
            O do not grinde me!

O do not fill me
20   With the turn'd viall of thy bitter wrath!
For thou hast other vessels full of bloud,
A part whereof my Saviour empti'd hath,
Ev'n unto death: since he di'd for my good,
            O do not kill me!

          But O reprieve me!
    For thou hast *life* and *death* at thy command;
    Thou art both *Judge* and *Saviour, feast* and *rod,*
    Cordiall and *Corrosive:* put not thy hand
    Into the bitter box; but O my God,
              My God, relieve me!

41

THE WORLD

Love built a stately house; where *Fortune* came,
And spinning phansies, she was heard to say,
That her fine cobwebs did support the frame,
Whereas they were supported by the same:
5   But *Wisdome* quickly swept them all away.

Then *Pleasure* came, who liking not the fashion,
Began to make *Balcones, Terraces,*
Till she had weakned all by alteration:
But rev'rend *laws,* and many a *proclamation*
10   Reformed all at length with menaces.

Then enter'd *Sinne,* and with that Sycomore,
Whose leaves first sheltred man from drought & dew,
Working and winding slily evermore,
The inward walls and Sommers cleft and tore:
15   But *Grace* shor'd these, and cut that as it grew.

Then *Sinne* combin'd with *Death* in a firm band
To rase the building to the very floore:
Which they effected, none could them withstand.
But *Love* and *Grace* took *Glorie* by the hand,
20   And built a braver Palace then before.

42

COLOSS. 3.3

OUR LIFE IS HID WITH CHRIST IN GOD.

My words & thoughts do both expresse this notion,
That *Life* hath with the sun a double motion.
The first *Is* straight, and our diurnall friend,
The other *Hid,* and doth obliquely bend.
One life is wrapt *In* flesh, and tends to earth.
The other winds towards *Him,* whose happie birth
Taught me to live here so, *That* still one eye
Should aim and shoot at that which *Is* on high:
Quitting with daily labour all *My* pleasure,
To gain at harvest an eternall *Treasure.*

43

VANITIE (1)

The fleet Astronomer can bore,
And thred the spheres with his quick-piercing minde:
He views their stations, walks from doore to doore,
Surveys, as if he had design'd
5   To make a purchase there: he sees their dances,
And knoweth long before,
Both their full-ey'd aspects, and secret glances.

The nimble Diver with his side
Cuts through the working waves, that he may fetch
10   His dearely-earned pearl, which God did hide
On purpose from the ventrous wretch;
That he might save his life, and also hers,
Who with excessive pride
Her own destruction and his danger wears.

15   The subtil Chymick can devest
And strip the creature naked, till he finde
The callow principles within their nest:
There he imparts to them his minde,
Admitted to their bed-chamber, before
20   They appear trim and drest
To ordinarie suitours at the doore.

What hath not man sought out and found,
But his deare God? who yet his glorious law
Embosomes in us, mellowing the ground
25   With showres and frosts, with love & aw,
So that we need not say, Where's this command?
        Poore man, thou searchest round
To finde out *death*, but missest *life* at hand.

44

VERTUE

Sweet day, so cool, so calm, so bright,
The bridall of the earth and skie:
The dew shall weep thy fall to night;
                    For thou must die.

5   Sweet rose, whose hue angrie and brave
Bids the rash gazer wipe his eye:
Thy root is ever in its grave,
                    And thou must die.

Sweet spring, full of sweet dayes and roses,
10   A box where sweets compacted lie;
My musick shows ye have your closes,
                    And all must die.

Onely a sweet and vertuous soul,
Like season'd timber, never gives;
15   But though the whole world turn to coal,
                    Then chiefly lives.

45

THE PEARL. *MATTH. 13.*

I know the wayes of learning; both the head
And pipes that feed the presse, and make it runne;
What reason hath from nature borrowed,
Or of it self, like a good huswife, spunne
5   In laws and policie; what the starres conspire,
What willing nature speaks, what forc'd by fire;
Both th' old discoveries, and the new-found seas,
The stock and surplus, cause and historie:
All these stand open, or I have the keyes:
10   Yet I love thee.

I know the wayes of honour, what maintains
The quick returns of courtesie and wit:
In vies of favours whether partie gains,
When glorie swells the heart, and moldeth it
15   To all expressions both of hand and eye,
Which on the world a true-love-knot may tie,
And bear the bundle, wheresoe're it goes:
How many drammes of spirit there must be
To sell my life unto my friends or foes:
20   Yet I love thee.

I know the wayes of pleasure, the sweet strains,
The lullings and the relishes of it;
The propositions of hot bloud and brains;
What mirth and musick mean; what love and wit
25   Have done these twentie hundred yeares, and more:
I know the projects of unbridled store:
My stuffe is flesh, not brasse; my senses live,
And grumble oft, that they have more in me
Then he that curbs them, being but one to five:
30   Yet I love thee.

I know all these, and have them in my hand.
Therefore not sealed, but with open eyes
I flie to thee, and fully understand
Both the main sale, and the commodities;
35   And at what rate and price I have thy love;
With all the circumstances that may move:
Yet through the labyrinths, not my groveling wit,
But thy silk twist let down from heav'n to me,
Did both conduct and teach me, how by it
40   To climbe to thee.

46

AFFLICTION (IV)

Broken in pieces all asunder,
   Lord, hunt me not,
   A thing forgot,
Once a poore creature, now a wonder,
   A wonder tortur'd in the space
   Betwixt this world and that of grace.

My thoughts are all a case of knives,
   Wounding my heart
   With scatter'd smart,
As watring pots give flowers their lives.
   Nothing their furie can controll,
   While they do wound and prick my soul.

All my attendants are at strife,
   Quitting their place
   Unto my face:
Nothing performs the task of life:
   The elements are let loose to fight,
   And while I live, trie out their right.

O help, my God! let not their plot
   Kill them and me,
   And also thee,
Who art my life: dissolve the knot,
   As the sunne scatters by his light
   All the rebellions of the night.

25 Then shall those powers, which work for grief,
                Enter thy pay,
                And day by day
    Labour thy praise, and my relief,
                With care and courage building me,
30   Till I reach heav'n, and much more thee.

47

MAN

My God, I heard this day,
That none doth build a stately habitation,
But he that means to dwell therein.
What house more stately hath there been,
5   Or can be, then is Man? to whose creation
All things are in decay.

For Man is ev'ry thing,
And more: He is a tree, yet bears no fruit;
A beast, yet is, or should be more:
10   Reason and speech we onely bring.
Parrats may thank us, if they are not mute,
They go upon the score.

Man is all symmetrie,
Full of proportions, one limbe to another,
15   And all to all the world besides:
Each part may call the farthest, brother:
For head with foot hath private amitie,
And both with moons and tides.

Nothing hath got so farre,
20   But Man hath caught and kept it, as his prey.
His eyes dismount the highest starre:
He is in little all the sphere.
Herbs gladly cure our flesh; because that they
Finde their acquaintance there.

72

25   For us the windes do blow,

The earth doth rest, heav'n move, and fountains flow.

Nothing we see, but means our good,

As our *delight*, or as our *treasure*:

The whole is, either our cupboard of *food*,

30   Or cabinet of *pleasure*.

The starres have us to bed;

Night draws the curtain, which the sunne withdraws;

Musick and light attend our head.

All things unto our *flesh* are kinde

35   In their *descent* and *being*; to our minde

In their *ascent* and *cause*.

Each thing is full of dutie:

Waters united are our navigation;

Distinguished, our habitation;

40   Below, our drink; above, our meat;

Both are our cleanlinesse. Hath one such beautie?

Then how are all things neat?

More servants wait on Man,

Then he'l take notice of: in ev'ry path

45   He treads down that which doth befriend him,

When sicknesse makes him pale and wan.

Oh mightie love! Man is one world, and hath

Another to attend him.

Since then, my God, thou hast

50   So brave a Palace built; O dwell in it,

That it may dwell with thee at last!

Till then, afford us so much wit;

That, as the world serves us, we may serve thee,

And both thy servants be.

48

UNKINDNESSE

Lord, make me coy and tender to offend:
In friendship, first I think, if that agree,
   Which I intend,
  Unto my friends intent and end.
5 I would not use a friend, as I use Thee.

If any touch my friend, or his good name;
It is my honour and my love to free
   His blasted fame
  From the least spot or thought of blame.
10 I could not use a friend, as I use Thee.

My friend may spit upon my curious floore:
Would he have gold? I lend it instantly;
   But let the poore,
  And thou within them starve at doore.
15 I cannot use a friend, as I use Thee.

When that my friend pretendeth to a place,
I quit my interest, and leave it free:
   But when thy grace
  Sues for my heart, I thee displace,
20 Nor would I use a friend, as I use Thee.

Yet can a friend what thou hast done fulfill?
O write in brasse, *My God upon a tree*
   His bloud did spill
  Onely to purchase my good-will:
25 *Yet use I not my foes, as I use thee.*

49

LIFE

I made a posie, while the day ran by:
Here will I smell my remnant out, and tie
$\qquad$ My life within this band.
But time did becken to the flowers, and they
5 By noon most cunningly did steal away,
$\qquad$ And wither'd in my hand.

My hand was next to them, and then my heart:
I took, without more thinking, in good part
$\qquad$ Times gentle admonition:
10 Who did so sweetly deaths sad taste convey,
Making my minde to smell my fatall day;
$\qquad$ Yet sugring the suspicion.

Farewell deare flowers, sweetly your time ye spent,
Fit, while ye liv'd, for smell or ornament,
15 $\qquad$ And after death for cures.
I follow straight without complaints or grief,
Since if my sent be good, I care not, if
$\qquad$ It be as short as yours.

50

AFFLICTION (V)

My God, I read this day,
That planted Paradise was not so firm,
As was and is thy floting Ark; whose stay
And anchor thou art onely, to confirm
     And strengthen it in ev'ry age,
     When waves do rise, and tempests rage.

At first we liv'd in pleasure;
Thine own delights thou didst to us impart:
When we grew wanton, thou didst use displeasure
To make us thine: yet that we might not part,
     As we at first did board with thee,
     Now thou wouldst taste our miserie.

There is but joy and grief;
If either will convert us, we are thine:
Some Angels us'd the first; if our relief
Take up the second, then thy double line
     And sev'rall baits in either kinde
     Furnish thy table to thy minde.

Affliction then is ours;
We are the trees, whom shaking fastens more,
While blustring windes destroy the wanton bowres,
And ruffle all their curious knots and store.
     My God, so temper joy and wo,
     That thy bright beams may tame thy bow.

51

MISERIE

Lord, let the Angels praise thy name.
Man is a foolish thing, a foolish thing,
    Folly and Sinne play all his game.
His house still burns, and yet he still doth sing,
5   *Man is but grasse,*
        He knows it, fill the glasse.

    How canst thou brook his foolishnesse?
Why he'l not lose a cup of drink for thee:
    Bid him but temper his excesse;
10   Not he: he knows, where he can better be,
            As he will swear,
        Then to serve thee in fear.

    What strange pollutions doth he wed,
And make his own? as if none knew, but he.
15   No man shall beat into his head,
That thou within his curtains drawn canst see:
            They are of cloth,
        Where never yet came moth.

    The best of men, turn but thy hand
20   For one poore minute, stumble at a pinne:
    They would not have their actions scann'd,
Nor any sorrow tell them that they sinne,
           Though it be small,
        And measure not their fall.

They quarrell thee, and would give over
The bargain made to serve thee: but thy love
  Holds them unto it, and doth cover
Their follies with the wing of thy milde Dove,
        Not suff'ring those
30   Who would, to be thy foes.

My God, Man cannot praise thy name:
Thou art all brightnesse, perfect puritie;
  The sunne holds down his head for shame,
Dead with eclipses, when we speak of thee:
35   How shall infection
        Presume on thy perfection?

As dirtie hands foul all they touch,
And those things most, which are most pure and fine:
  So our clay hearts, ev'n when we crouch
40 To sing thy praises, make them lesse divine.
          Yet either this,
        Or none thy portion is.

Man cannot serve thee; let him go,
And serve the swine: there, there is his delight:
45 He doth not like this vertue, no;
Give him his dirt to wallow in all night:
          These Preachers make
        His head to shoot and ake.

Oh foolish man! where are thine eyes?
50 How hast thou lost them in a croud of cares?
Thou pull'st the rug, and wilt not rise,
No not to purchase the whole pack of starres:
There let them shine,
Thou must go sleep, or dine.

55 The bird that sees a daintie bowre
Made in the tree, where she was wont to sit,
Wonders and sings, but not his power
Who made the arbour: this exceeds her wit.
But Man doth know
60 The spring, whence all things flow:

And yet as though he knew it not,
His knowledge winks, and lets his humours reigne;
They make his life a constant blot,
And all the bloud of God to run in vain.
65 Ah wretch! what verse
Can thy strange wayes rehearse?

Indeed at first Man was a treasure,
A box of jewels, shop of rarities,
A ring, whose posie was, *My pleasure:*
70 He was a garden in a Paradise:
Glorie and grace
Did crown his heart and face.

But sinne hath fool'd him. Now he is
A lump of flesh, without a foot or wing
                To raise him to the glimpse of blisse:
A sick toss'd vessel, dashing on each thing;
                        Nay, his own shelf:
                My God, I mean my self.

52

JORDAN (II)

When first my lines of heav'nly joyes made mention,
Such was their lustre, they did so excell,
That I sought out quaint words, and trim invention;
My thoughts began to burnish, sprout, and swell,
5   Curling with metaphors a plain intention,
Decking the sense, as if it were to sell.

Thousands of notions in my brain did runne,
Off'ring their service, if I were not sped:
I often blotted what I had begunne;
10   This was not quick enough, and that was dead.
Nothing could seem too rich to clothe the sunne,
Much lesse those joyes which trample on his head.

As flames do work and winde, when they ascend,
So did I weave my self into the sense.
15   But while I bustled, I might heare a friend
Whisper, *How wide is all this long pretence !*
There is in love a sweetnesse readie penn'd :
Copie out onely that, and save expense.

53

SION

Lord, with what glorie wast thou serv'd of old,
When Solomons temple stood and flourished!
      Where most things were of purest gold;
      The wood was all embellished
With flowers and carvings, mysticall and rare:
All show'd the builders, crav'd the seers care.

Yet all this glorie, all this pomp and state
Did not affect thee much, was not thy aim;
      Something there was, that sow'd debate:
      Wherefore thou quitt'st thy ancient claim:
And now thy Architecture meets with sinne;
For all thy frame and fabrick is within.

There thou art struggling with a peevish heart,
Which sometimes crosseth thee, thou sometimes it:
      The fight is hard on either part.
      Great God doth fight, he doth submit.
All Solomons sea of brasse and world of stone
Is not so deare to thee as one good grone.

And truly brasse and stones are heavie things,
Tombes for the dead, not temples fit for thee:
      But grones are quick, and full of wings,
      And all their motions upward be;
And ever as they mount, like larks they sing;
The note is sad, yet musick for a king.

54

HOME

Come Lord, my head doth burn, my heart is sick,
  While thou dost ever, ever stay:
Thy long deferrings wound me to the quick,
  My spirit gaspeth night and day.
5   O shew thy self to me,
    Or take me up to thee!

How canst thou stay, considering the pace
  The bloud did make, which thou didst waste?
When I behold it trickling down thy face,
10 I never saw thing make such haste.
    O show thy self to me,
    Or take me up to thee!

When man was lost, thy pitie lookt about
  To see what help in th' earth or skie:
15 But there was none; at least no help without:
  The help did in thy bosome lie.
    O show thy self to me,
    Or take me up to thee!

There lay thy sonne: and must he leave that nest,
20 That hive of sweetnesse, to remove
Thraldome from those, who would not at a feast
  Leave one poore apple for thy love?
    O show thy self to me,
    Or take me up to thee!

25 He did, he came: O my Redeemer deare,
              After all this canst thou be strange?
So many yeares baptiz'd, and not appeare?
              As if thy love could fail or change.
                        O show thy self to me,
30   Or take me up to thee!

Yet if thou stayest still, why must I stay?
              My God, what is this world to me?
This world of wo? hence all ye clouds, away,
              Away; I must get up and see.
35   O show thy self to me,
                        Or take me up to thee!

What is this weary world; this meat and drink,
              That chains us by the teeth so fast?
What is this woman-kinde, which I can wink
40   Into a blacknesse and distaste?
                        O show thy self to me,
                        Or take me up to thee!

With one small sigh thou gav'st me th' other day
              I blasted all the joyes about me:
45 And scouling on them as they pin'd away,
              Now come again, said I, and flout me.
                        O show thy self to me,
                        Or take me up to thee!

Nothing but drought and dearth, but bush and brake,
50   Which way so-e're I look, I see.
Some may dream merrily, but when they wake,
          They dresse themselves and come to thee.
                    O show thy self to me,
                    Or take me up to thee!

55   We talk of harvests; there are no such things,
          But when we leave our corn and hay:
There is no fruitfull yeare, but that which brings
          The last and lov'd, though dreadfull day.
                    O show thy self to me,
60   Or take me up to thee!

Oh loose this frame, this knot of man untie!
          That my free soul may use her wing,
Which now is pinion'd with mortalitie,
          As an intangled, hamper'd thing.
65   O show thy self to me,
                    Or take me up to thee!

What have I left, that I should stay and grone?
          The most of me to heav'n is fled:
My thoughts and joyes are all packt up and gone,
70   And for their old acquaintance plead.
                    O show thy self to me,
                    Or take me up to thee!

Come dearest Lord, passe not this holy season,
My flesh and bones and joynts do pray:
75 And ev'n my verse, when by the ryme and reason
The word is, *Stay*, sayes ever, *Come*.
O show thy self to me,
Or take me up to thee!

55

THE BRITISH CHURCH

I joy, deare Mother, when I view
Thy perfect lineaments, and hue
      Both sweet and bright.

Beautie in thee takes up her place,
And dates her letters from thy face,
      When she doth write.

A fine aspect in fit aray,
Neither too mean, nor yet too gay,
      Shows who is best.

Outlandish looks may not compare:
For all they either painted are,
      Or else undrest.

She on the hills, which wantonly
Allureth all in hope to be
      By her preferr'd,

Hath kiss'd so long her painted shrines,
That ev'n her face by kissing shines,
      For her reward.

She in the valley is so shie
Of dressing, that her hair doth lie
      About her eares:

While she avoids her neighbours pride,
She wholly goes on th' other side,
                    And nothing wears.

25   But dearest Mother, (what those misse)
The mean thy praise and glorie is,
                    And long may be.

Blessed be God, whose love it was
To double-moat thee with his grace,
30   And none but thee.

56

THE QUIP

The merrie world did on a day
With his train-bands and mates agree
To meet together, where I lay,
And all in sport to geere at me.

5   First, Beautie crept into a rose,
Which when I pluckt not, Sir, said she,
Tell me, I pray, Whose hands are those?
But thou shalt answer, Lord, for me.

Then Money came, and chinking still,
10   What tune is this, poore man? said he:
I heard in Musick you had skill.
But thou shalt answer, Lord, for me.

Then came brave Glorie puffing by
In silks that whistled, who but he?
15   He scarce allow'd me half an eie.
But thou shalt answer, Lord, for me.

Then came quick Wit and Conversation
And he would needs a comfort be,
And, to be short, make an oration.
20   But thou shalt answer, Lord, for me.

Yet when the houre of thy designe
To answer these fine things shall come;
Speak not at large, say, I am thine:
And then they have their answer home.

57

THE DAWNING

Awake sad heart, whom sorrow ever drowns;
    Take up thine eyes, which feed on earth;
Unfold thy forehead gather'd into frowns:
    Thy Saviour comes, and with him mirth:
5   Awake, awake;
And with a thankfull heart his comforts take.
    But thou dost still lament, and pine, and crie;
    And feel his death, but not his victorie.

Arise sad heart; if thou dost not withstand,
10   Christs resurrection thine may be:
Do not by hanging down break from the hand,
    Which as it riseth, raiseth thee:
                   Arise, arise;
And with his buriall-linen drie thine eyes:
15   Christ left his grave-clothes, that we might, when grief
    Draws tears, or bloud, not want an handkerchief.

58

JESU

JESU is in my heart, his sacred name
Is deeply carved there: but th'other week
A great affliction broke the little frame,
Ev'n all to pieces: which I went to seek:
And first I found the corner, where was *J*,
After, where *E S*, and next where *U* was graved.
When I had got these parcels, instantly
I sat me down to spell them, and perceived
That to my broken heart he was *I ease you*,
                    And to my whole is *J E S U*.

59

DULNESSE

※

Why do I languish thus, drooping and dull,
                    As if I were all earth?
O give me quicknesse, that I may with mirth
                    Praise thee brim-full!

5   The wanton lover in a curious strain
                    Can praise his fairest fair;
And with quaint metaphors her curled hair
                    Curl o're again.

Thou art my lovelinesse, my life, my light,
10   Beautie alone to me:
Thy bloudy death and undeserv'd, makes thee
                    Pure red and white.

When all perfections as but one appeare,
                    That those thy form doth show;
15   The very dust, where thou dost tread and go,
                    Makes beauties here;

Where are my lines then? my approaches? views?
                    Where are my window-songs?
Lovers are still pretending, & ev'n wrongs
20   Sharpen their Muse:

But I am lost in flesh, whose sugred lyes
                Still mock me, and grow bold:
Sure thou didst put a minde there, if I could
                    Finde where it lies.

25   Lord, cleare thy gift, that with a constant wit
                I may but look towards thee:
Look onely; for to *love* thee, who can be,
                  What angel fit?

60

LOVE-JOY

As on a window late I cast mine eye,
I saw a vine drop grapes with *J* and *C*
Anneal'd on every bunch. One standing by
Ask'd what it meant. I (who am never loth
To spend my iudgement) said, It seem'd to me
To be the bodie and the letters both
Of *Joy* and *Charitie*. Sir, you have not miss'd,
The man reply'd; It figures *JESUS CHRIST*.

61

FROM PROVIDENCE

O sacred Providence, who from end to end
Strongly and sweetly movest! shall I write,
And not of thee, through whom my fingers bend
To hold my quill? shall they not do thee right?

5   Of all the creatures both in sea and land
Onely to Man thou hast made known thy wayes,
And put the penne alone into his hand,
And made him Secretarie of thy praise.

Beasts fain would sing; birds dittie to their notes;
10   Trees would be tuning on their native lute
To thy renown: but all their hands and throats
Are brought to Man, while they are lame and mute.

Man is the worlds high Priest: he doth present
The sacrifice for all; while they below
15   Unto the service mutter an assent,
Such as springs use that fall, and windes that blow.

He that to praise and laud thee doth refrain,
Doth not refrain unto himself alone,
But robs a thousand who would praise thee fain,
20   And doth commit a world of sinne in one.

The beasts say, Eat me: but, if beasts must teach,
The tongue is yours to eat, but mine to praise.
The trees say, Pull me: but the hand you stretch,
Is mine to write, as it is yours to raise.

25 Wherefore, most sacred Spirit, I here present
For me and all my fellows praise to thee:
And just it is that I should pay the rent,
Because the benefit accrues to me.

We all acknowledge both thy power and love
30 To be exact; transcendent, and divine;
Who dost so strongly and so sweetly move,
While all things have their will, yet none but thine.

For either thy *command,* or thy *permission*
Lay hands on all: they are thy *right* and *left.*
35 The first puts on with speed and expedition;
The other curbs sinnes stealing pace and theft.

Nothing escapes them both; all must appeare,
And be dispos'd, and dress'd, and tun'd by thee,
Who sweetly temper'st all. If we could heare
40 Thy skill and art, what musick would it be!

Thou art in small things great, not small in any:
Thy even praise can neither rise, nor fall.
Thou art in all things one, in each thing many:
For thou art infinite in one and all.

. . .

Each creature hath a wisdome for his good.
The pigeons feed their tender off-spring, crying,
When they are callow; but withdraw their food
When they are fledge, that need may teach them flying.

65   Bees work for man; and yet they never bruise
Their masters flower, but leave it, having done,
As fair as ever, and as fit to use;
So both the flower doth stay, and hony run.

Sheep eat the grasse, and dung the ground for more:
70   Trees after bearing drop their leaves for soil:
Springs vent their streams, and by expense get store:
Clouds cool by heat, and baths by cooling boil.

. . .

Thy creatures leap not, but expresse a feast,
Where all the guests sit close, and nothing wants.
135   Frogs marry fish and flesh; bats, bird and beast;
Sponges, non-sense and sense; mines, th' earth & plants.

To show thou art not bound, as if thy lot
Were worse then ours; sometimes thou shiftest hands.
Most things move th' under-jaw; the Crocodile not.
140   Most things sleep lying; th' Elephant leans or stands.

But who hath praise enough? nay who hath any?
None can expresse thy works, but he that knows them;
And none can know thy works, which are so many,
And so complete, but onely he that owes them.

145 All things that are, though they have sev'rall wayes,
  Yet in their being joyn with one advise
  To honour thee: and so I give thee praise
  In all my other hymnes, but in this twice.

  Each thing that is, although in use and name
150 It go for one, hath many wayes in store
  To honour thee; and so each hymne thy fame
  Extolleth many wayes, yet this one more.
  Lines quoted are 1–44, 61–72, 133–52

62

HOPE

❧

I gave to Hope a watch of mine: but he
        An anchor gave to me.
Then an old prayer-book I did present:
        And he an optick sent.
With that I gave a viall full of tears:
        But he a few green eares:
Ah Loyterer! I'le no more, no more I'le bring:
        I did expect a ring.

63

SINNES ROUND

Sorrie I am, my God, sorrie I am,
That my offences course it in a ring.
My thoughts are working like a busie flame,
Untill their cockatrice they hatch and bring:
And when they once have perfected their draughts,
My words take fire from my inflamed thoughts.

My words take fire from my inflamed thoughts,
Which spit it forth like the Sicilian hill.
They vent the wares, and passe them with their faults,
And by their breathing ventilate the ill.
But words suffice not, where are lewd intentions:
My hands do joyn to finish the inventions.

My hands do joyn to finish the inventions:
And so my sinnes ascend three stories high,
As Babel grew, before there were dissentions.
Yet ill deeds loyter not: for they supplie
New thoughts of sinning: wherefore, to my shame,
Sorrie I am, my God, sorrie I am.

64

GRATEFULNESSE

Thou that hast giv'n so much to me,
Give one thing more, a gratefull heart.
See how thy beggar works on thee
           By art.

He makes thy gifts occasion more,
And sayes, If he in this be crost,
All thou hast giv'n him heretofore
           Is lost.

But thou didst reckon, when at first
Thy word our hearts and hands did crave,
What it would come to at the worst
           To save.

Perpetuall knockings at thy doore,
Tears sullying thy transparent rooms,
Gift upon gift, much would have more,
           And comes.

This not withstanding, thou wentst on,
And didst allow us all our noise:
Nay thou hast made a sigh and grone
           Thy joyes.

Not that thou hast not still above
Much better tunes, then grones can make;
But that these countrey-aires thy love
Did take.

25 Wherefore I crie, and crie again;
And in no quiet canst thou be,
Till I a thankfull heart obtain
Of thee:

30 Not thankfull, when it pleaseth me;
As if thy blessings had spare dayes:
But such a heart, whose pulse may be
Thy praise.

65

PEACE

Sweet Peace, where dost thou dwell? I humbly crave,
                    Let me once know.
        I sought thee in a secret cave,
            And ask'd, if Peace were there.
5   A hollow winde did seem to answer, No:
                  Go seek elsewhere.

I did; and going did a rainbow note:
                  Surely, thought I,
        This is the lace of Peaces coat:
10   I will search out the matter.
But while I lookt, the clouds immediately
                Did break and scatter.

Then went I to a garden, and did spy
                  A gallant flower,
15   The crown Imperiall: Sure, said I,
            Peace at the root must dwell.
But when I digg'd, I saw a worm devoure
                What show'd so well.

At length I met a rev'rend good old man,
20   Whom when for Peace
        I did demand; he thus began:
            There was a Prince of old
At Salem dwelt, who liv'd with good increase
                Of flock and fold.

25 He sweetly liv'd; yet sweetnesse did not save
                              His life from foes.
          But after death out of his grave
                    There sprang twelve stalks of wheat:
     Which many wondring at, got some of those
30   To plant and set.

     It prosper'd strangely, and did soon disperse
                         Through all the earth:
          For they that taste it do rehearse,
               That vertue lies therein,
35   A secret vertue bringing peace and mirth
                         By flight of sinne.

     Take of this grain, which in my garden grows,
                         And grows for you;
          Make bread of it: and that repose
                         And peace which ev'ry where
40   With so much earnestnesse you do pursue,
                         Is onely there.

66

THE BUNCH OF GRAPES

Joy, I did lock thee up: but some bad man
          Hath let thee out again:
And now, me thinks, I am where I began
          Sev'n yeares ago: one vogue and vein,
5   One aire of thoughts usurps my brain.
I did toward Canaan draw; but now I am
Brought back to the Red sea, the sea of shame.

For as the Jews of old by Gods command
          Travell'd, and saw no town:
10 So now each Christian hath his journeys spann'd:
          Their storie pennes and sets us down.
          A single deed is small renown.
Gods works are wide, and let in future times;
His ancient justice overflows our crimes.

15 Then have we too our guardian fires and clouds;
          Our Scripture-dew drops fast:
We have our sands and serpents, tents and shrowds;
          Alas! our murmurings come not last.
          But where's the cluster? where's the taste
20 Of mine inheritance? Lord, if I must borrow,
Let me as well take up their joy, as sorrow.

But can he want the grape, who hath the wine?
                    I have their fruit and more.
Blessed be God, who prosper'd *Noahs* vine,
                        And made it bring forth grapes good store.
                    But much more him I must adore,
Who of the laws sowre juice sweet wine did make,
Ev'n God himself, being pressed for my sake.

67

LOVE UNKNOWN

Deare Friend, sit down, the tale is long and sad:
And in my faintings I presume your loue
Will more complie, then help. A Lord I had,
And have, of whom some grounds which may improve,
I hold for two lives, and both lives in me.
To him I brought a dish of fruit one day,
And in the middle plac'd my heart. But he
                              (I sigh to say)
Lookt on a seruant, who did know his eye
Better then you know me, or (which is one)
Then I my self. The servant instantly
Quitting the fruit, seiz'd on my heart alone,
And threw it in a font, wherein did fall
A stream of bloud, which issu'd from the side
Of a great rock: I well remember all,
And have good cause: there it was dipt and di'd,
And washt, and wrung: the very wringing yet
Enforceth tears. *Your heart was foul, I fear.*
Indeed 'tis true. I did and do commit
Many a fault more then my lease will bear;
Yet still askt pardon, and was not deni'd.
But you shall heare. After my heart was well,
And clean and fair, as I one even-tide
                              (I sigh to tell)
Walkt by my self abroad, I saw a large
And spacious fornace flaming, and thereon
A boyling caldron, round about whose verge
Was in great letters set *AFFLICTION.*

The greatnesse shew'd the owner. So I went
To fetch a sacrifice out of my fold,
Thinking with that, which I did thus present,
To warm his love, which I did fear grew cold.
But as my heart did tender it, the man
Who was to take it from me, slipt his hand,
And threw my heart into the scalding pan;
My heart, that brought it (do you understand?)
The offerers heart. *Your heart was hard, I fear.*
Indeed 'tis true. I found a callous matter
Began to spread and to expatiate there:
But with a richer drug, then scalding water,
I bath'd it often, ev'n with holy bloud,
Which at a board, while many drunk bare wine,
A friend did steal into my cup for good,
Ev'n taken inwardly, and most divine
To supple hardnesses. But at the length
Out of the caldron getting, soon I fled
Unto my house, where to repair the strength
Which I had lost, I hasted to my bed.
But when I thought to sleep out all these faults
                              (I sigh to speak)
I found that some had stuff'd the bed with thoughts,
I would say *thorns*. Deare, could my heart not break,
When with my pleasures ev'n my rest was gone?
Full well I understood, who had been there:
For I had giv'n the key to none, but one:
It must be he. *Your heart was dull, I fear.*
Indeed a slack and sleepie state of minde
Did oft possesse me, so that when I pray'd,
Though my lips went, my heart did stay behinde.
But all my scores were by another paid,
Who took the debt upon him. *Truly, Friend,*

For ought I heare, your Master shows to you
More favour then you wot of. Mark the end.
The Font did onely, what was old, renew:
65   The Caldron suppled, what was grown too hard:
The Thorns did quicken, what was grown too dull:
All did but strive to mend, what you had marr'd.
Wherefore be cheer'd, and praise him to the full
Each day, each houre, each moment of the week,
70   Who fain would have you be, new, tender, quick.

68

MANS MEDLEY

Heark, how the birds do sing,
   And woods do ring.
All creatures have their joy: and man hath his.
  Yet if we rightly measure,
    Mans joy and pleasure
Rather hereafter, then in present, is.

  To this life things of sense
    Make their pretence:
In th' other Angels have a right by birth:
    Man ties them both alone,
     And makes them one,
With th' one hand touching heav'n, with th' other earth.

  In soul he mounts and flies,
    In flesh he dies.
He wears a stuffe whose thread is course and round,
   But trimm'd with curious lace,
    And should take place
After the trimming, not the stuffe and ground.

  Not, that he may not here
    Taste of the cheer,
But as birds drink, and straight lift up their head,
   So must he sip and think
    Of better drink
He may attain to, after he is dead.

25 But as his joyes are double;
                So is his trouble.
    He hath two winters, other things but one:
                Both frosts and thoughts do nip,
                            And bite his lip;
30 And he of all things fears two deaths alone.

                Yet ev'n the greatest griefs
                        May be reliefs,
    Could he but take them right, and in their wayes.
                Happie is he, whose heart
35   Hath found the art
    To turn his double pains to double praise.

69

PARADISE

I blesse thee, Lord, because I GROW
Among thy trees, which in a ROW
To thee both fruit and order OW.

What open force, or hidden CHARM
Can blast my fruit, or bring me HARM,
While the inclosure is thine ARM?

Inclose me full for fear I START.
Be to me rather sharp and TART,
Then let me want thy hand & ART.

When thou dost greater judgements SPARE,
And with thy knife but prune and PARE,
Ev'n fruitfull trees more fruitfull ARE.

Such sharpnes shows the sweetest FREND:
Such cuttings rather heal then REND:
And such beginnings touch their END.

70

EPHES. 4.30
GRIEVE NOT THE HOLY SPIRIT, ETC.

And art thou grieved, sweet and sacred Dove,
>> When I am sowre,
>> And crosse thy love?
> Grieved for me? the God of strength and power
5 >> Griev'd for a worm, which when I tread,
>> I passe away and leave it dead?

Then weep mine eyes, the God of love doth grieve:
>> Weep foolish heart,
>> And weeping live:
10 For death is drie as dust. Yet if ye part,
>> End as the night, whose sable hue
>> Your sinnes expresse; melt into dew.

When sawcie mirth shall knock or call at doore,
>> Cry out, Get hence,
15 >> Or cry no more.
Almightie God doth grieve, he puts on sense:
>> I sinne not to my grief alone,
>> But to my Gods too; he doth grone.

Oh take thy lute, and tune it to a strain,
20 >> Which may with thee
>> All day complain.
There can no discord but in ceasing be.
>> Marbles can weep; and surely strings
>> More bowels have, then such hard things.

Lord, I adjudge my self to tears and grief,
   Ev'n endlesse tears
    Without relief.
If a cleare spring for me no time forbears,
   But runnes, although I be not drie;
   I am no Crystall, what shall I?

Yet if I wail not still, since still to wail
   Nature denies;
    And flesh would fail,
If my deserts were masters of mine eyes:
   Lord, pardon, for thy sonne makes good
   My want of tears with store of bloud.

71

THE PILGRIMAGE

I travell'd on, seeing the hill, where lay
   My expectation.
  A long it was and weary way.
   The gloomy cave of Desperation
5 I left on th' one, and on the other side
   The rock of Pride.

And so I came to phansies medow strow'd
   With many a flower:
  Fain would I here have made abode,
10   But I was quicken'd by my houre.
So to cares cops I came, and there got through
   With much ado.

That led me to the wilde of passion, which
   Some call the wold;
15   A wasted place, but sometimes rich.
   Here I was robb'd of all my gold,
Save one good Angell, which a friend had ti'd
   Close to my side.

At length I got unto the gladsome hill,
20   Where lay my hope,
   Where lay my heart; and climbing still,
   When I had gain'd the brow and top,
A lake of brackish waters on the ground
   Was all I found.

With that abash'd and struck with many a sting
　　　　　　Of swarming fears,
　　　　I fell, and cry'd, Alas my King;
　　　　　Can both the way and end be tears?
Yet taking heart I rose, and then perceiv'd
　　　　　　I was deceiv'd:

My hill was further: so I flung away,
　　　　　　Yet heard a crie
　　　　Just as I went, *None goes that way*
　　　　And lives: If that be all, said I,
After so foul a journey death is fair,
　　　　　　And but a chair.

72

THE HOLDFAST

I threatned to observe the strict decree
        Of my deare God with all my power & might.
        But I was told by one, it could not be;
Yet I might trust in God to be my light.

5   Then will I trust, said I, in him alone.
        Nay, ev'n to trust in him, was also his:
        We must confesse, that nothing is our own.
Then I confesse that he my succour is:

But to have nought is ours, not to confesse
10   That we have nought. I stood amaz'd at this,
        Much troubled, till I heard a friend expresse,
That all things were more ours by being his.
        What Adam had, and forfeited for all,
        Christ keepeth now, who cannot fail or fall.

73

PRAISE (II)

King of Glorie, King of Peace,
        I will love thee:
And that love may never cease,
        I will move thee.

Thou hast granted my request,
        Thou hast heard me:
Thou didst note my working breast,
        Thou hast spar'd me.

Wherefore with my utmost art
        I will sing thee,
And the cream of all my heart
        I will bring thee.

Though my sinnes against me cried,
        Thou didst cleare me;
And alone, when they replied,
        Thou didst heare me.

Sev'n whole dayes, not one in seven,
        I will praise thee.
In my heart, though not in heaven,
        I can raise thee.

Thou grew'st soft and moist with tears,
       Thou relentedst:
And when Justice call'd for fears,
       Thou dissentedst.

25   Small it is, in this poore sort
          To enroll thee:
Ev'n eternitie is too short
          To extoll thee.

74

LONGING

With sick and famisht eyes,
With doubling knees and weary bones,
To thee my cries,
To thee my grones,
To thee my sighs, my tears ascend:
No end?

My throat, my soul is hoarse:
My heart is wither'd like a ground
Which thou dost curse.
My thoughts turn round,
And make me giddie; Lord, I fall,
Yet call.

From thee all pitie flows.
Mothers are kinde, because thou art,
And dost dispose
To them a part:
Their infants, them; and they suck thee
More free.

Bowels of pitie, heare!
Lord of my soul, love of my minde,
Bow down thine eare!
Let not the winde
Scatter my words, and in the same
Thy name!

25   Look on my sorrows round!
    Mark well my furnace! O what flames,
             What heats abound!
             What griefs, what shames!
    Consider, Lord; Lord, bow thine eare,
30   And heare!

         Lord Jesu, thou didst bow
    Thy dying head upon the tree:
             O be not now
             More dead to me!
35   Lord heare! *Shall he that made the eare,*
              Not heare?

         Behold, thy dust doth stirre,
    It moves, it creeps, it aims at thee:
             Wilt thou deferre
40   To succour me,
    Thy pile of dust, wherein each crumme
             Sayes, Come?

         To thee help appertains.
    Hast thou left all things to their course,
             And laid the reins
45   Upon the horse?
    Is all lockt? hath a sinners plea
             No key?

         Indeed the world's thy book,
50   Where all things have their leafe assign'd:
             Yet a meek look
             Hath interlin'd.
    Thy board is full, yet humble guests
             Finde nests.

55 Thou tarriest, while I die,
And fall to nothing: thou dost reigne,
    And rule on high,
    While I remain
In bitter grief: yet am I stil'd
60   Thy childe.

    Lord, didst thou leave thy throne,
Not to relieve? how can it be,
    That thou art grown
    Thus hard to me?
65 Were sinne alive, good cause there were
          To bear.

    But now both sinne is dead,
And all thy promises live and bide.
    That wants his head;
70   These speak and chide,
And in thy bosome poure my tears,
          As theirs.

    Lord J E S U, heare my heart,
Which hath been broken now so long,
75   That ev'ry part
    Hath got a tongue!
Thy beggars grow; rid them away
          To day.

    My love, my sweetnesse, heare!
80 By these thy feet, at which my heart
    Lies all the yeare,
    Pluck out thy dart,
And heal my troubled breast which cryes,
          Which dyes.

THE COLLAR

I struck the board, and cry'd, No more.
                    I will abroad.
        What? shall I ever sigh and pine?
My lines and life are free; free as the rode,
5   Loose as the winde, as large as store.
                    Shall I be still in suit?
            Have I no harvest but a thorn
            To let me bloud, and not restore
    What I have lost with cordiall fruit?
10   Sure there was wine
                Before my sighs did drie it: there was corn
                Before my tears did drown it.
            Is the yeare onely lost to me?
                Have I no bayes to crown it?
15   No flowers, no garlands gay? all blasted?
                            All wasted?
        Not so, my heart: but there is fruit,
                            And thou hast hands.
                Recover all thy sigh-blown age
20 On double pleasures: leave thy cold dispute
Of what is fit, and not forsake thy cage,
                            Thy rope of sands,
    Which pettie thoughts have made, and made to thee
            Good cable, to enforce and draw,
25   And be thy law,
        While thou didst wink and wouldst not see.
                    Away; take heed:
                    I will abroad.

Call in thy deaths head there: tie up thy fears.

30
                              He that forbears
            To suit and serve his need,
                        Deserves his load.
But as I rav'd and grew more fierce and wilde
                        At every word,
35   Me thoughts I heard one calling, *Childe:*
            And I reply'd, *My Lord.*

76

THE CALL

Come, my Way, my Truth, my Life:
Such a Way, as gives us breath:
Such a Truth, as ends all strife:
And such a Life, as killeth death.

5   Come, my Light, my Feast, my Strength:
Such a Light, as shows a feast:
Such a Feast, as mends in length:
Such a Strength, as makes his guest.

       Come, my Joy, my Love, my Heart:
10   Such a Joy, as none can move:
Such a Love, as none can part:
Such a Heart, as joyes in love.

77

CLASPING OF HANDS

Lord, thou art mine, and I am thine,
If mine I am: and thine much more,
Then I or ought, or can be mine.
Yet to be thine, doth me restore;
So that again I now am mine,
And with advantage mine the more:
Since this being mine, brings with it thine,
And thou with me dost thee restore.
   If I without thee would be mine,
   I neither should be mine nor thine.

Lord, I am thine, and thou art mine:
So mine thou art, that something more
I may presume thee mine, then thine.
For thou didst suffer to restore
Not thee, but me, and to be mine:
And with advantage mine the more,
Since thou in death wast none of thine,
Yet then as mine didst me restore.
   O be mine still! still make me thine!
   Or rather make no Thine and Mine!

78

THE PULLEY

When God at first made man,
Having a glasse of blessings standing by;
Let us (said he) poure on him all we can:
Let the worlds riches, which dispersed lie,
5   Contract into a span.

So strength first made a way;
Then beautie flow'd, then wisdome, honour, pleasure:
When almost all was out, God made a stay,
Perceiving that alone of all his treasure
10   Rest in the bottome lay.

For if I should (said he)
Bestow this jewell also on my creature,
He would adore my gifts in stead of me,
And rest in Nature, not the God of Nature:
15   So both should losers be.

Yet let him keep the rest,
But keep them with repining restlesnesse:
Let him be rich and wearie, that at least,
If goodnesse leade him not, yet wearinesse
20   May tosse him to my breast.

79

THE PRIESTHOOD

Blest Order, which in power dost so excell,
That with th' one hand thou liftest to the sky,
And with the other throwest down to hell
In thy just censures; fain would I draw nigh,
5   Fain put thee on, exchanging my lay-sword
              For that of th' holy word.

But thou art fire, sacred and hallow'd fire;
And I but earth and clay: should I presume
To wear thy habit, the severe attire
10   My slender compositions might consume.
    I am both foul and brittle; much unfit
              To deal in holy Writ.

Yet have I often seen, by cunning hand
And force of fire, what curious things are made
15   Of wretched earth. Where once I scorn'd to stand,
    That earth is fitted by the fire and trade
    Of skilfull artists, for the boards of those
              Who make the bravest shows.

But since those great ones, be they ne're so great,
20   Come from the earth, from whence those vessels come;
    So that at once both feeder, dish, and meat
    Have one beginning and one finall summe:
    I do not greatly wonder at the sight,
              If earth in earth delight.

25   But th' holy men of God such vessels are,
     As serve him up, who all the world commands:
     When God vouchsafeth to become our fare,
     Their hands conuey him, who conveys their hands.
     O what pure things, most pure must those things be,
30   Who bring my God to me!

     Wherefore I dare not, I, put forth my hand
     To hold the Ark, although it seem to shake
     Through th' old sinnes and new doctrines of our land.
     Onely, since God doth often vessels make
35   Of lowly matter for high uses meet,
                    I throw me at his feet.

     There will I lie, untill my Maker seek
     For some mean stuffe whereon to show his skill:
     Then is my time. The distance of the meek
40   Doth flatter power. Lest good come short of ill
     In praising might, the poore do by submission
                  What pride by opposition.

80

GRIEF

O who will give me tears? Come all ye springs,
Dwell in my head & eyes: come clouds, & rain:
My grief hath need of all the watry things,
That nature hath produc'd. Let ev'ry vein
5 Suck up a river to supply mine eyes,
My weary weeping eyes too drie for me,
Unlesse they get new conduits, new supplies
To bear them out, and with my state agree.
What are two shallow foords, two little spouts
10 Of a lesse world? the greater is but small,
A narrow cupboard for my griefs and doubts,
Which want provision in the midst of all.
Verses, ye are too fine a thing, too wise
For my rough sorrows: cease, be dumbe and mute,
15 Give up your feet and running to mine eyes,
And keep your measures for some lovers lute,
Whose grief allows him musick and a ryme:
For mine excludes both measure, tune, and time.
                                    Alas, my God!

81

THE CROSSE

What is this strange and uncouth thing?
To make me sigh, and seek, and faint, and die,
Untill I had some place, where I might sing,
    And serve thee; and not onely I,
5   But all my wealth, and familie might combine
To set thy honour up, as our designe.

And then when after much delay,
Much wrastling, many a combate, this deare end,
So much desir'd, is giv'n, to take away
10   My power to serve thee; to unbend
All my abilities, my designes confound,
And lay my threatnings bleeding on the ground.

One ague dwelleth in my bones,
Another in my soul (the memorie
15   What I would do for thee, if once my grones
    Could be allow'd for harmonie)
I am in all a weak disabled thing,
Save in the sight thereof, where strength doth sting.

Besides, things sort not to my will,
20   Ev'n when my will doth studie thy renown:
Thou turnest th' edge of all things on me still,
    Taking me up to throw me down:
So that, ev'n when my hopes seem to be sped,
I am to grief alive, to them as dead.

To have my aim, and yet to be
Farther from it then when I bent my bow,
To make my hopes my torture, and the fee
    Of all my woes another wo,
Is in the midst of delicates to need,
And ev'n in Paradise to be a weed.

    Ah my deare Father, ease my smart!
These contrarieties crush me: these crosse actions
Doe winde a rope about, and cut my heart:
    And yet since these thy contradictions
Are properly a crosse felt by thy sonne,
With but foure words, my words, *Thy will be done.*

82

THE FLOWER

How fresh, O Lord, how sweet and clean
Are thy returns! ev'n as the flowers in spring;
    To which, besides their own demean,
The late-past frosts tributes of pleasure bring.
5   Grief melts away
               Like snow in May,
    As if there were no such cold thing.

    Who would have thought my shrivel'd heart
Could have recover'd greennesse? It was gone
10   Quite under ground; as flowers depart
To see their mother-root, when they have blown;
               Where they together
               All the hard weather,
    Dead to the world, keep house unknown.

15   These are thy wonders, Lord of power,
Killing and quickning, bringing down to hell
    And up to heaven in an houre;
Making a chiming of a passing-bell.
               We say amisse,
20   This or that is:
    Thy word is all, if we could spell.

O that I once past changing were,
Fast in thy Paradise, where no flower can wither!
Many a spring I shoot up fair,
Offring at heav'n, growing and groning thither:
Nor doth my flower
Want a spring-showre,
My sinnes and I joining together:

But while I grow in a straight line,
Still upwards bent, as if heav'n were mine own,
Thy anger comes, and I decline:
What frost to that? what pole is not the zone,
Where all things burn,
When thou dost turn,
And the least frown of thine is shown?

And now in age I bud again,
After so many deaths I live and write;
I once more smell the dew and rain,
And relish versing: O my onely light,
It cannot be
That I am he
On whom thy tempests fell all night.

These are thy wonders, Lord of love,
To make us see we are but flowers that glide:
Which when we once can finde and prove,
Thou hast a garden for us, where to bide.
Who would be more,
Swelling through store,
Forfeit their Paradise by their pride.

83

Let forrain nations of their language boast,
What fine varietie each tongue affords:
I like our language, as our men and coast:
Who cannot dresse it well, want wit, not words.
5   How neatly doe we give one onely name
To parents issue and the sunnes bright starre!
A sonne is light and fruit; a fruitfull flame
Chasing the fathers dimnesse, carri'd farre
From the first man in th' East, to fresh and new
10   Western discov'ries of posteritie.
So in one word our Lords humilitie
We turn upon him in a sense most true:
            For what Christ once in humblenesse began,
            We him in glorie call, *The Sonne of Man.*

84

A TRUE HYMNE

My joy, my life, my crown!
My heart was meaning all the day,
   Somewhat it fain would say:
And still it runneth mutt'ring up and down
5   With onely this, *My joy, my life, my crown.*

   Yet slight not these few words:
   If truly said, they may take part
      Among the best in art.
The finenesse which a hymne or psalme affords,
10   Is, when the soul unto the lines accords.

   He who craves all the minde,
   And all the soul, and strength, and time,
      If the words onely ryme,
Justly complains, that somewhat is behinde
15   To make his verse, or write a hymne in kinde.

   Whereas if th' heart be moved,
   Although the verse be somewhat scant,
      God doth supplie the want.
As when th' heart sayes (sighing to be approved)
20   *O, could I love* ! and stops: God writeth, *Loved.*

85

BITTER-SWEET

Ah my deare angrie Lord,
Since thou dost love, yet strike;
Cast down, yet help afford;
Sure I will do the like.

5 I will complain, yet praise;
I will bewail, approve:
And all my sowre-sweet dayes
I will lament, and love.

86

THE GLANCE

When first thy sweet and gracious eye
Vouchsaf 'd ev'n in the midst of youth and night
To look upon me, who before did lie
                Weltring in sinne;
5   I felt a sugred strange delight,
Passing all cordials made by any art,
Bedew, embalme, and overrunne my heart,
                And take it in.

        Since that time many a bitter storm
10   My soul hath felt, ev'n able to destroy,
Had the malicious and ill-meaning harm
                His swing and sway:
But still thy sweet originall joy
Sprung from thine eye, did work within my soul,
15   And surging griefs, when they grew bold, controll;
                And got the day.

        If thy first glance so powerfull be,
A mirth but open'd and seal'd up again;
What wonders shall we feel, when we shall see
20   Thy full-ey'd love!
When thou shalt look us out of pain,
And one aspect of thine spend in delight
More then a thousand sunnes disburse in light,
                In heav'n above.

87

THE 23 PSALME

The God of love my shepherd is,
  And he that doth me feed:
While he is mine, and I am his,
  What can I want or need?

5 He leads me to the tender grasse,
  Where I both feed and rest;
Then to the streams that gently passe:
  In both I have the best.

Or if I stray, he doth convert
10 And bring my minde in frame:
And all this not for my desert,
  But for his holy name.

Yea, in deaths shadie black abode
  Well may I walk, not fear:
15 For thou art with me; and thy rod
  To guide, thy staffe to bear.

Nay, thou dost make me sit and dine,
  Ev'n in my enemies sight:
My head with oyl, my cup with wine
20 Runnes over day and night.

Surely thy sweet and wondrous love
  Shall measure all my dayes;
And as it never shall remove,
  So neither shall my praise.

88

AARON

※

Holinesse on the head,
Light and perfections on the breast,
Harmonious bells below, raising the dead
To leade them unto life and rest.
5   Thus are true Aarons drest.

Profanenesse in my head,
Defects and darknesse in my breast,
A noise of passions ringing me for dead
Unto a place where is no rest.
10   Poore priest thus am I drest.

Onely another head
I have, another heart and breast,
Another musick, making live not dead,
Without whom I could have no rest:
15   In him I am well drest.

Christ is my onely head,
My alone onely heart and breast,
My onely musick, striking me ev'n dead;
That to the old man I may rest,
20   And be in him new drest.

So holy in my head,
Perfect and light in my deare breast,
My doctrine tun'd by Christ, (who is not dead,
But lives in me while I do rest)
25   Come people; Aaron's drest.

89

THE ODOUR, 2. COR. 2

How sweetly doth *My Master* sound! *My Master*!
　　As Amber-greese leaves a rich sent
　　　　Unto the taster:
　　So do these words a sweet content,
5　An orientall fragrancie, *My Master*.

With these all day I do perfume my minde,
　　My minde ev'n thrust into them both;
　　　　That I might finde
　　What cordials make this curious broth,
10　This broth of smells, that feeds and fats my minde.

My Master, shall I speak? O that to thee
　　My servant were a little so,
　　　　As flesh may be;
　　That these two words might creep & grow
15　To some degree of spicinesse to thee!

Then should the Pomander, which was before
　　A speaking sweet, mend by reflection,
　　　　And tell me more:
　　For pardon of my imperfection
20　Would warm and work it sweeter then before.

For when *My Master*, which alone is sweet,
　　And ev'n in my unworthinesse pleasing,
　　　　Shall call and meet,
　　My servant, as thee not displeasing,
25　That call is but the breathing of the sweet.

This breathing would with gains by sweetning me
   (As sweet things traffick when they meet)
    Return to thee.
  And so this new commerce and sweet
30 Should all my life employ, and busie me.

90

THE FORERUNNERS

The harbingers are come. See, see their mark;
White is their colour, and behold my head.
But must they have my brain? Must they dispark
Those sparkling notions, which therein were bred?
5   Must dulnesse turn me to a clod?
Yet have they left me, *Thou art still my God.*

Good men ye be, to leave me my best room,
Ev'n all my heart, and what is lodged there:
I passe not, I, what of the rest become,
10   So *Thou art still my God,* be out of fear.
        He will be pleased with that dittie;
And if I please him, I write fine and wittie.

Farewell sweet phrases, lovely metaphors.
But will ye leave me thus? when ye before
15   Of stews and brothels onely knew the doores,
Then did I wash you with my tears, and more,
        Brought you to Church well drest and clad:
My God must have my best, ev'n all I had.

Louely enchanting language, sugar-cane,
20   Hony of roses, whither wilt thou flie?
Hath some fond lover tic'd thee to thy bane?
And wilt thou leave the Church, and love a stie?
        Fie, thou wilt soil thy broider'd coat,
And hurt thy self, and him that sings the note.

25 Let foolish lovers, if they will love dung,
With canvas, not with arras clothe their shame:
Let follie speak in her own native tongue.
True beautie dwells on high: ours is a flame
            But borrow'd thence to light us thither.
30 Beautie and beauteous words should go together.

Yet if you go, I passe not; take your way:
For, *Thou art still my God*, is all that ye
Perhaps with more embellishment can say.
Go birds of spring: let winter have his fee,
35   Let a bleak palenesse chalk the doore,
So all within be livelier then before.

91

DISCIPLINE

Throw away thy rod,
Throw away thy wrath:
       Oh my God,
Take the gentle path.

5   For my hearts desire
Unto thine is bent:
       I aspire
To a full consent.

Not a word or look
10   I affect to own,
       But by book,
And thy book alone.

Though I fail, I weep:
Though I halt in pace,
15   Yet I creep
To the throne of grace.

Then let wrath remove;
Love will do the deed:
       For with love
20   Stonie hearts will bleed.

Love is swift of foot;
Love's a man of warre,
       And can shoot,
And can hit from farre.

Who can scape his bow?
That which wrought on thee,
　　　　Brought thee low,
Needs must work on me.

Throw away thy rod;
Though man frailties hath,
　　　　Thou art God:
Throw away thy wrath.

92

THE INVITATION

Come ye hither all, whose taste
                    Is your waste;
Save your cost, and mend your fare.
God is here prepar'd and drest,
                    And the feast,
God, in whom all dainties are.

Come ye hither all, whom wine
                    Doth define,
Naming you not to your good:
Weep what ye have drunk amisse,
                    And drink this,
Which before ye drink is bloud.

Come ye hither all, whom pain
                    Doth arraigne,
Bringing all your sinnes to sight:
Taste and fear not: God is here
                    In this cheer,
And on sinne doth cast the fright.

Come ye hither all, whom joy
                    Doth destroy,
While ye graze without your bounds:
Here is joy that drowneth quite
                    Your delight,
As a floud the lower grounds.

Come ye hither all, whose love
                              Is your dove,
And exalts you to the skie:
Here is love, which having breath
                              Ev'n in death,
After death can never die.

Lord I have invited all,
                              And I shall
Still invite, still call to thee:
For it seems but just and right
                              In my sight,
Where is all, there all should be.

93

THE POSIE

Let wits contest,
And with their words and posies windows fill:
Lesse then the least
Of all thy mercies, is my posie still.

5   This on my ring,
This by my picture, in my book I write:
Whether I sing,
Or say, or dictate, this is my delight.

Invention rest,
10   Comparisons go play, wit use thy will:
Lesse then the least
Of all Gods mercies, is my posie still.

94

A PARODIE

꙰

Souls joy, when thou art gone,
And I alone,
Which cannot be,
Because thou dost abide with me,
5   And I depend on thee;

Yet when thou dost suppresse
The cheerfulnesse
Of thy abode,
And in my powers not stirre abroad,
10   But leave me to my load:

O what a damp and shade
Doth me invade!
No stormie night
Can so afflict or so affright,
15   As thy eclipsed light.

Ah Lord! do not withdraw,
Lest want of aw
Make Sinne appeare;
And when thou dost but shine lesse cleare,
20   Say, that thou art not here.

And then what life I have,
While sinne doth rave,
And falsly boast,
That I may seek, but thou art lost;
25   Thou and alone thou know'st.

O what a deadly cold
Doth me infold!
I half beleeve,
That Sinne sayes true: but while I grieve,
Thou com'st and dost relieve.

30

95

THE ELIXER

Teach me, my God and King,
In all things thee to see,
And what I do in any thing,
To do it as for thee:

5   Not rudely, as a beast,
To runne into an action;
But still to make thee prepossest,
And give it his perfection.

A man that looks on glasse,
10   On it may stay his eye;
Or if he pleaseth, through it passe,
And then the heav'n espie.

All may of thee partake:
Nothing can be so mean,
15   Which with his tincture (for thy sake)
Will not grow bright and clean.

A servant with this clause
Makes drudgerie divine:
Who sweeps a room, as for thy laws,
20   Makes that and th' action fine.

This is the famous stone
That turneth all to gold:
For that which God doth touch and own
Cannot for lesse be told.

96

A WREATH

A wreathed garland of deserved praise,
Of praise deserved, unto thee I give,
I give to thee, who knowest all my wayes,
My crooked winding wayes, wherein I live,
Wherein I die, not live: for life is straight,
Straight as a line, and ever tends to thee,
To thee, who art more farre above deceit,
Then deceit seems above simplicitie.
Give me simplicitie, that I may live,
So live and like, that I may know thy wayes,
Know them and practise them: then shall I give
For this poore wreath, give thee a crown of praise.

97

DEATH

Death, thou wast once an uncouth hideous thing,
         Nothing but bones,
      The sad effect of sadder grones:
Thy mouth was open, but thou couldst not sing.

5   For we consider'd thee as at some six
         Or ten yeares hence,
      After the losse of life and sense,
Flesh being turn'd to dust, and bones to sticks.

We lookt on this side of thee, shooting short;
10   Where we did finde
      The shells of fledge souls left behinde,
Dry dust, which sheds no tears, but may extort.

But since our Saviours death did put some bloud
         Into thy face;
15   Thou art grown fair and full of grace,
Much in request, much sought for, as a good.

For we do now behold thee gay and glad,
         As at dooms-day;
      When souls shall wear their new aray,
20 And all thy bones with beautie shall be clad.

Therefore we can go die as sleep, and trust
         Half that we have
      Unto an honest faithfull grave;
Making our pillows either down, or dust.

98

DOOMS-DAY

Come away,
Make no delay.
Summon all the dust to rise,
Till it stirre, and rubbe the eyes;
While this member jogs the other,
Each one whispring, *Live you brother?*

Come away,
Make this the day.
Dust, alas, no musick feels,
But thy trumpet: then it kneels,
As peculiar notes and strains
Cure Tarantulaes raging pains.

Come away,
O make no stay!
Let the graves make their confession,
Lest at length they plead possession:
Fleshes stubbornnesse may have
Read that lesson to the grave.

Come away,
Thy flock doth stray.
Some to windes their bodie lend,
And in them may drown a friend:
Some in noisome vapours grow
To a plague and publick wo.

Come away,
                             Help our decay.
                     Man is out of order hurl'd,
                     Parcel'd out to all the world.
                     Lord, thy broken consort raise,
And the musick shall be praise.

HEAVEN

O who will show me those delights on high?
    Echo.   *I.*
Thou Echo, thou art mortall, all men know.
    Echo.   *No.*
5 Wert thou not born among the trees and leaves?
    Echo.   *Leaves.*
And are there any leaves, that still abide?
    Echo.   *Bide.*
What leaves are they? impart the matter wholly.
10   *Echo.*   *Holy.*
Are holy leaves the Echo then of blisse?
    Echo.   *Yes.*
Then tell me, what is that supreme delight?
    Echo.   *Light.*
15 Light to the minde: what shall the will enjoy?
    Echo.   *Joy.*
But are there cares and businesse with the pleasure?
    Echo.   *Leisure.*
Light, joy, and leisure; but shall they persever?
20   *Echo.*   *Ever.*

LOVE (III)

Love bade me welcome: yet my soul drew back,
          Guiltie of dust and sinne.
But quick-ey'd Love, observing me grow slack
          From my first entrance in,
5   Drew nearer to me, sweetly questioning,
          If I lack'd any thing.

A guest, I answer'd, worthy to be here:
          Love said, you shall be he.
I the unkinde, ungratefull? Ah my deare,
10   I cannot look on thee.
Love took my hand, and smiling did reply,
          Who made the eyes but I?

Truth Lord, but I have marr'd them: let my shame
          Go where it doth deserve.
15 And know you not, sayes Love, who bore the blame?
          My deare, then I will serve.
You must sit down, sayes Love, and taste my meat:
          So I did sit and eat.

FINIS.
Glorie be to God on high, and on earth
peace, good will towards men.

Glossary

abroach: 'to set abroach', to pierce a hole in a wine cask

ague: intense fever

Amber-greese: ambergris, a wax-like substance used in perfumery

anneal: burn colours into glass

arraigne: accuse publicly

arras: rich tapestry fabric

assay: put to the test

bane: hapless fate, ruin

begirt: surround, enclose

behither: except for

betimes: before it is too late

calcined: burnt, reduced to ashes

cavil: dispute, make objection without good reason

chaw: chew roughly

Chymick: chemist; also, in the seventeenth century, alchemist

close [noun]: cadence, the conclusion of a musical phrase

cockatrice: mythical serpent-like creature associated with sin

consort [noun]: a small group of musicians playing instruments of the same kind; a 'broken consort' brought together instruments of different kinds

crazie: full of cracks or flaws

curious: delicate, fine; ingenious

demean: bearing, demeanour; also a legal term ('demesne', pronounced as 'demean') for estate or dominion

disburse: pay out

disseized: wrongfully dispossessed

diurnall: daily

doom: the Day of Judgment

enroll: celebrate, write in the roll of honour

extoll: magnify, raise high with praise

H.: abbreviation of Holy

handsell: first instalment, foretaste

harbinger: forerunner, herald

Ieat: jet, black marble

leaven [noun]: fermenting dough

Lidger: resident ambassador

magazen: storehouse

momentanie: momentary

optick: telescope (an 'optic glass')

outlandish: foreign

outwork: outer fortification

passing-bell: tolling funeral bell (indicating that someone has 'passed' on)

Pomander: ball of aromatic substances tightly packed together, which when warmed or rubbed gives a stronger perfume

prevent: go before, anticipate

Prime: the winning position in the card game 'Primero'

purling: rippling, bubbling

quick [adjective]: alive

quicknesse: vitality, the quality of being 'quick'

quidditie: over-subtle quibble; also, the essence of things

rent [verb]: tear

smart [noun]: pain, suffering

Sommers: supporting beams

spittle: hospital

standing [noun]: standing-place, position of residence

suppling: softening, rendering supple

thraldome: enslavement

tincture: dye; also, alchemical term for a spiritual principle infused into material things

ventrous: adventurous

viall: glass vessel for liquids; a 'turn'd viall' has rounded edges

weal: welfare, happiness

wormwood: bitter medicine

Sources

George Herbert's poems exist in three versions: an early, incomplete manuscript which includes some corrections in Herbert's own hand (MS Jones B 62, dating from *c.* 1620, at Dr Williams's Library, London); a complete presentation manuscript copied out by the women of the Little Gidding community (MS Tanner 307, *c.* 1633, at the Bodleian Library, Oxford); and the first edition set by the printers to Cambridge University, Thomas Buck and Roger Daniel (Cambridge, 1633). The text of this selection of Herbert's poems is based on the 1633 edition in its original spelling and layout, and is taken from *The English Poems of George Herbert*, edited by Helen Wilcox (Cambridge University Press, 2007). For extensive annotation and critical discussion of the individual poems, as well as an index of biblical references and an annotated interpretative glossary of important recurring words in Herbert's poetry, readers are referred to this fuller edition.

Index of titles

Index of first lines

My heart did heave, and there came forth, *O God!*, 50
My joy, my life, my crown!, 136
My stock lies dead, and no increase, 38
My words & thoughts do both expresse this notion, 64

Not in rich furniture, or fine aray, 25

O blessed bodie! Whither art thou thrown?, 13
O do not use me, 61
O my chief good, 10
O sacred Providence, who from end to end, 95
O who will give me tears? Come all ye springs, 130
O who will show me those delights on high?, 157
Oh all ye, who passe by, whose eyes and minde, 3
Oh Book! infinite sweetnesse! let my heart, 34
Oh glorious spirits, who after all your bands, 53
Oh King of grief! (a title strange, yet true, 7
Oh that I knew how all thy lights combine, 34

Peace mutt'ring thoughts, and do not grudge to keep, 47
Philosophers have measur'd mountains, 9
Prayer the Churches banquet, Angels age, 24

Rise heart; thy Lord is risen. Sing his praise, 14

Since, Lord, to thee, 17
Sorrie I am, my God, sorrie I am, 100
Souls joy, when thou art gone, 150
Sweet day, so cool, so calm, so bright, 67
Sweetest of sweets, I thank you: when displeasure, 43
Sweet Peace, where dost thou dwell? I humbly crave, 103

Teach me, my God and King, 152
The fleet Astronomer can bore, 65
The God of love my shepherd is, 139
The harbingers are come. See, see their mark, 143
The merrie world did on a day, 89